AUTISM
From Tragedy
to Triumph

Carol Johnson
and
Julia Crowder

BRANDEN BOOKS
Branden Publishing Company, Inc.

Library of Congress Cataloging-in-Publication Data

Johnson, Carol (Carol Sue)
    Autism : from tragedy to triumph / Carol Johnson
and Julia Crowder.
                p. cm.
    Includes bibliographical references and index.
    ISBN 0-8283-1965-0
    1. Crowder, Drew.
    2. Autistic children--United States--Biography.
    3. Autistic children--Rehabilitation--Case studies.
    4. Autistic children--Education--Case studies.
    5. Parents of autistic children--Case studies.
I. Crowder, Julia. II. Title.
    RJ506.A9J64   1994
    618.92'8982'0092--dc20   94-2118
    [B]   CIP

BRANDEN PUBLISHING COMPANY
17 Station Street
Box 843 Brookline Village
Boston, MA 02147

CONTENTS

Foreword by Dr. O. Ivar Lovaas 5
Part I: The Long Road to Diagnosis 13
    Chapter 1 14
    Chapter 2 27
    Chapter 3 30
    Chapter 4 34
    Chapter 5 46
    Chapter 6 52
    Chapter 7 62
    Chapter 8 67
Part II: Treatment 85
    Chapter 9--Parent Therapy Log 86
    Chapter 10 93
    Chapter 11--Clinic Therapy Log 97
    Chapter 12 112
    Chapter 13 128
    Chapter 14--Therapy Log 139
    Chapter 15--Parent Therapy Log 153
    Chapter 16 162
    Chapter 17 164
    Chapter 18 170
    Chapter 19 174
    Chapter 20 177
Afterword 179
Glossary 184

This book is dedicated to Jim, Sally, the Spraker Workshop, and all the others who believed in me when I didn't believe in myself. (CJ) To Dr. O. Ivar Lovaas and Dr. Andrea Ackerman for their guidance and support, and to Laurie, Howard, Martha and Richard, volunteers in the fight for Drew's life. Thank you for your time, and most importantly, for your love. We won. (JC)

Foreword

by

Ivar Lovaas, Ph.D.

In this book Julia Crowder describes her efforts in the treatment and education of her son, Drew, who was once diagnosed with autism. Julia describes, as only a mother can, the fears and confusions a parent feels when told that there is something seriously wrong with their young child and in all likelihood, their problem is so severe that it cannot be corrected with available treatments, and to anticipate and be prepared for the child's life-long institutionalization.

Julia began her search for an effective treatment with many disadvantages. She was poor, she was on the verge of divorce, she had responsibility for two other children, and she lived in Los Angeles, where she had no family, and was essentially alone. In 1975, when Julia contacted our clinic, very little was known about how to help children like Drew, and we could not even provide an estimate of what the chances were for improvements with the treatment we were able to offer. Finally, off and on during treatment, Julia would express guilt and lay much blame upon herself for Drew having failed to develop. Somehow or other, she felt that she must have done something wrong, otherwise Drew would not have the problems he now evidenced. Bettelheim's destructive theory about parental causation was well known. Today, there is no support for his position.

Julia had the strength to face all these problems--she was rich in a way that would never make her poor. As a parent-therapist for her child, she learned a great deal about how to teach Drew a quite complex task. She had to help administer and supervise a group of student therapists, she had to help pick the right kind of school for her son and establish a constructive relationship with his teachers, and so on. On top of that, Julia went on to college, entered the school of special education and later obtained certification as a speech therapist.

I mention these accomplishments because many would be led to believe, that faced with the kinds of problems which Julia encountered, one would be likely to give up and just try to escape. While such an outcome is possible, in the history of the clinic, this is the exception rather than the rule. More often than not we see mothers like Julia who grow and develop when given information about how to help their children improve. In fact, it is the parents of children like Drew who have pioneered new forms of treatment and in a way led the profession in constructive directions.

To enjoy the company of parents like Julia makes one's work with developmentally disabled children a meaningful learning experience. And when one has the pleasure of helping treat a child like Drew, whose progress in treatment was so steady and rapid, then one has been doubly rewarded.

At this point it is important to point out that the diagnosis of autism, which Drew received when he was three years of age, points to a very heterogeneous group of children. Intake (pre-treatment) examination does not predict with any certainty how any one child will progress in treatment. About half of the children that have been treated in the UCLA Psychology

Department's Autism Clinic show normal functioning at follow-up, but the other half remain developmentally delayed and in all likelihood will retain a diagnosis of autism as adults. When Dr. Leo Kanner first suggested the diagnosis, he considered such children to be recoverable. This was then followed by a period during which a professional climate suggested the condition to be chronic and irreversible. Over the last few years, there is evidence that some children can be helped to recover.

In regard to Drew, Julia presents her story very well and I may add to the following observations. The question may be raised whether Drew was in fact "autistic". Perhaps he was misdiagnosed and that Julia's story really is a misleading story in the sense that Drew would have gotten better without treatment. If this was the case, all the work that Julia had done would be to no avail, and her story would not help other parents and children who receive such a diagnosis. I will emphatically answer such a charge by stating that, according to Drew's independent diagnosis and our own observations, Drew fulfilled all the criteria of one having autism.

Julia began to suspect that something was wrong with Drew when he was 9 months old at which time she thought he was hearing impaired because he would not orient towards her when she spoke to him. Already as an infant, he liked it best when he was alone and would not cry, even when hurt. In fact Julia had to check Drew all the time because he would not give any signs that he was hurt or missed anybody. He had "funny movements of his eyes" in that he would gaze at objects through the corners of his eyes, he would jump up and down in one spot or run back and forth from one point in the house to the other. He would line objects in neat rows and feel their surfaces with his fingers. He would sift sand and he did not have any speech. He showed little or no appropriate toy play, and most significantly, he did not play with other children. On the positive side he would occasionally echo words, and he had some self-help skills in that he was toilet-trained, could partly dress himself, and eat unassisted. Also, he did not have an excessive amount of tantrums. His intake IQ (on the Bayley Scale) was 61, placing him in the mildly retarded range of intellectual functioning.

If a young child, like Drew, was diagnosed with autism and scored in the mildly retarded range on a commonly used IQ test, then one can safely predict that, without early and intensive behavioral treatment, the child's condition would not change over time. Follow-up studies of such children show IQ scores to remain essentially the same or be somewhat lower as they grow older, and the diagnosis of autism would either be maintained or changed to mental retardation or chronic schizophrenia.

Drew's progress in treatment was relatively rapid and an examination of his gains on normed and well established tests will reflect this. It is important to note that these assessments were given by professionals who were not a part of Drew's treatment, did not know his history and were independent of the UCLA clinic. Drew obtained a Bayley's IQ of 61 when he was three years old. Over the next year and a half Drew made rapid progress in all areas of treatment and when administered the Wechsler Preschool and Primary Scale of Intelligence at four and a half years of age, he obtained an IQ score of 100. It is of interest to note that, at that time, his scores on the performance items exceeded his scores on the verbal part of the scale, consistent with the diagnosis of autism. However, at the same time he had an examination by a speech patholo-gist who assessed his language to fall within the normal limits and to "not warrant speech therapy at this time". When Drew was retested at 8 years of age on the Wechsler Intelligence Scale for Children, his full scale IQ was 120, with a verbal IQ of 125 exceeding his performance IQ of 108. He scored higher than 90 percent of children his own age, within the "superior range of intellectual functioning". Of particular interest for a child like Drew, with the earlier diagnosis of autism, is an examination of the scale scores which indicate understanding of social relationships, such as the picture arrangement and comprehension subscales. Drew scored above average on these. In 1984 when he was 12 years of age, he was tested by his school district because he was suspected to be gifted. He was then in the 5th grade. His scores on the various subtests of the Woodcock-Johnson battery show that no scale score fell below the 92 percentile and on scales of learning, motivation, creativity and leadership, his scores were all consistent with the ratings of a gifted student. To quote the conclusion of the examiner: "Drew demonstrated no social and emotional behaviors which could negatively effect his academic development."

The diagnosis of autism involves placing individuals in discrete, qualitatively different categories. A more helpful approach, which also is more in line with scien-tific data, is to view individuals as different in degrees rather than kind. This may come about because our nervous systems, which mediate all learning, are all different. Most of us are, by definition born with "average" nervous systems in the sense that the day-to-day (average) environment helps us learn. That environment does not teach that well to persons like Drew, and his mother can attest to that. This necessitates the development and testing of special environments to help such persons learn. At the same time, it is important to keep in mind that we must help develop and encourage variability among and within persons, because of the survival value, artistic and scientific contributions contributed by such variance.

There will be an increasingly large number of children who, like Drew, will receive early and intensive behavioral intervention. It is important to make two warnings at this point: First, there exist no license-requirements to call oneself a behavior therapist and in fact there are a number of persons who claim that they can provide behavioral treatment without knowing a great deal about such treatment of children with autism and/or developmental disabilities. About 80 percent of intensive behavioral treatment with young children is focused on helping the children develop more meaningful language. The requirement of teaching language, to mention just one area, requires that the provider of treatment knows how to teach a variety of skills, from helping mute children acquire verbal imitation, to teaching abstract language such as pronouns, prepositions, and time concepts. Finally, the therapist/teacher has to teach the child how to talk and play with normal peers. Indeed, very few professionals can provide such treatment at this point, and none can provide it without prior training. (It is possible to acquire the skills in 6 to 12 months of supervised apprenticeship).

The second warning pertains to the outcome of treatment. Drew received 40 or more hours of 1:1 treatment per week between the ages of three and five. it is unlikely that this kind of treatment will work that successfully with children much above the age of five, or with children who would receive less than 30 hours a week of 1:1 treatment. Furthermore, only half of the children who treated will gain what we have labelled as "normal functioning".

There are certain references which may be helpful for further reading. One of these is a teaching manual, "Teaching Developmentally Disabled Children, the Me Book," which can be obtained by writing Pro-Ed Company, 8700 Shoal Creek Blvd., Austin, Texas 78758-6897. The book may also be ordered by phone by calling (512) 451-3246. Description of the treatment outcome data of the Young Autism Project, in which Drew participated, is provided in the following publications:

1. Lovaas, O.I. (1987). Behavioral treatment and normal educational and intellectual functioning in young autistic children. Journal of consulting and Clinical Psychology, 55, 3-9.

2. McEachin, J.J., Smith, T. & Lovaas, O.I. (1993). Long-term outcome for children with autism who received early intensive behavioral treatment. American Journal on Mental Retardation, 97 (4), 359-372.

For more information about autism in general contact Bernard Rimland, Ph.D. Institute for Child Behavior Research, 4128 Adams Ave., San Diego, CA 92116.

For more information about the Young Autism Project, contact Ivar Lovaas, Ph.D., Department of Psychology, University of California, Los Angeles, CA. 90014, telephone: (310) 825-2319.

Part 1

The Long Road To Diagnosis

Chapter 1

Eh-h, eh-hh, eh-h." The nasal sound of Drew's demand for breakfast preceded him into the kitchen. I scurried about, intent on setting food of some kind in front of my youngest son before his demands escalated. I plopped a bowl of Cream of Wheat on the formica table.

"Eh-h, eh-h, eh-hh, EH-HHH," Drew intoned.

John, my four-year-old, sat across the table from Drew and picked Cheerios one by one from a half-full bowl of milk. His left elbow was propped on the table, and he pointed at Drew with his two week old Christmas present, a small friction-powered sports car. "Pow!" he said, pretending the car was a gun. He blew imaginary smoke from the imaginary gun barrel. "He wants raisins in it," he told me.

"We're out of raisins," I said, as I stirred a pat of butter, a little sugar and some milk into the hot cereal, and squinted through the smoke that drifted up from my cigarette.

John looked at me, then shrugged and returned to his Cheerios. "Drew's not gonna like that," he informed me.

I sighed. Just this once, I thought, just this once, no raisins. Even as the thought skittered across my mind, the loudness and intensity of Drew's demand increased.

I removed the cigarette from my mouth and blew on a spoonful of raisin-less Cream of Wheat.

"Come on, Honey," I coaxed. "Try it." I tried to feed it to him, but he twisted his face away from the spoon with a grimace.

"Eh-h, eh-h, eh-h, eh-h-h-h-HHHH," he cried. With each utterance, the growl grew closer to a shriek.

"Please, Drew, just one bite. Mommy's out of raisins, okay? Just one--"

"Drew wants raisins," John said again.

"Mom, I can't find my other shoe." Marie's voice drifted into the kitchen, and she soon followed. "Mom! Listen to me. Jenny is going to be here in a minute. I have to find my shoe or we'll be late for Sunday School."

I looked to where she stood on one bare foot, holding a white Ked by its laces.

"I need--"

"Honey, you'll have to hold on just a minute." I gritted my teeth and tried to hold Drew's head with one hand and put the spoon to his lips with the other. "Come on, just one little bite," I muttered.

With all the stubbornness of any other nearly-three-year-old, he clenched his own teeth and twisted his head away from the spoon. "Eh-h, Eh-h, EH-H, EH-H," he said, and the nasal whine finally realized its full potential and became a shriek.

Exasperated, I banged the spoon down in his bowl and went to the telephone. Drew rocked back and forth, but the shrieks had been reduced to a monotonous "Eh-h, eh-h, eh-h." He shoved the bowl across the table to where John sat.

"Huh-uh," John said, and shoved the bowl back across the table to Drew as I waited for my next door neighbor to answer the phone.

"Mom, please," Marie said, at my elbow now. "I have to find my shoe. I looked every--"

I laid my hand on her arm. "Just a sec, ok? I'll--oh, Marilyn, thank God you're home," I said as the phone was picked up on the other end. I heard her yawn.

"Yeah. I try to never go anywhere until after I'm out of bed."

"Do you have any raisins?" I asked, one eye on the Cream of Wheat as it traveled back and forth across the table. John enjoyed the game, but Drew seemed to view it as just another facet of the desperate rites he followed each day.

"Um, raisins?" Marilyn yawned again. "Yeah, I think so."

"I'll send John over," I said, hung up the phone and shuffled after Marie to help her find her missing shoe. Here it was not even nine in the morning and I was nearly worn out already.

Marie and I located her missing shoe just as her friend Jenny rang the doorbell. Marie stuck her foot in the shoe, called a hasty good bye, and left for Sunday School.

I trudged back to the kitchen, and John banged in the back door with a small box of raisins. He gave them to me then ran down the hall to the room he shared with Drew.

I dumped some raisins into Drew's Cream of Wheat, and he picked up his spoon. "It's probably cold by now," I said. Drew made no response. He simply began to eat. I sighed, and followed John to help him dress.

As I slipped a T-shirt over his head, I said, "You can go outside and play, but you have to stay in the fence, ok?"

John looked up at me, his bright black eyes like buttons. "I always stay in the fence," he said. "Marie don't, though, 'cause she goes to school."

"That's right," I said. "Another year and you can go to school, too."

He stood on one foot while I slipped his shorts over the other and pulled them up to his waist. "How long is a year?"

"A long time. When you have another birthday it will be almost time for you to go to school." I worked his shoes onto his feet and tied them.

"Does Drew get to go to school with me?"

"No." I made up the bunk beds, then turned to John. "Why don't you go on outside now?"

Instead, he climbed the bunk beds' ladder until he stood nearly eye to eye with me. "Will you make Drew come outside and play with me?"

"Honey, go on outside, ok? You know I can't make Drew play with you."

"But I want him to. I don't have nobody to play with," he whined. He got on the top bunk on his knees and whacked the bed with both open palms. "Why do I have to have a brother that won't play with me?" He whacked the bed again.

I lifted him from the bed, kissed his forehead, and set him on his feet. "I don't know, John. I wish I did."

He left the room without his customary bounce, and I heard the back door slam. I went into the kitchen, and found Drew still at the table. Half his cereal remained in his bowl. If I wanted him out of the kitchen by lunch, I had to help him along. Left on his own, he chewed each bite 30 or 40 times, even something with the mushy consistency of Cream of Wheat.

I flipped the portable television on and took the spoon from him. I spooned cereal into his mouth and idly kept track of the early-Sunday morning shows on the television. "Medix" came on, and I watched it with little interest at first.

Suddenly, I froze with the spoon poised in mid-air. The camera panned a large room full of children and finally zoomed in on a child about Drew's age who spun a large plastic lid over and over again, gaze riveted to it. That image gave way to one of a child who rocked back and forth, and recited a litany of seemingly meaningless sounds. The camera moved once more and I saw a little girl who wore a helmet and repeatedly banged her head into a wall. My eyes remained on the screen until I heard Drew's own stream of meaningless sounds: "Eh-eh-eh," he said, eyes on the spoon poised in the air in front of him.

I looked at him, and pieces of his short life ran through my mind in jerky sequence, like faulty film on a movie screen: Drew as he stared through and around people, never meeting their gaze; his aversion to being cuddled, first as an infant, and now as a toddler; his lack of response to most stimuli outside the walls of ritual that surrounded him; his frantic insistence on adherence to that ritual; his failure to develop any significant language skills.

I looked back to the television screen. A name and number flashed across the screen, and I dropped the spoon to scrabble frantically for a pencil and paper. "Dr. Laura Schreibman, 555-1023," I muttered as I looked for a writing instrument. Finally, I found a laundry marker in the bottom of a desk drawer, and scribbled the number on a grocery sack. I ignored Drew's increasingly loud shrieks for the moment and stared at the number I had written down.

I was not the type of person to fall for any miracle cures, but I knew that somewhere, there must be an answer to whatever was really wrong with my son. Could this finally be the answer I had searched for? Could Drew be autistic? Panic bubbled up from within as I sorted through the information stored in my mind, residue of the dozens of books I'd read in my quest for the basis of Drew's behavior. Autism. Did that mean retarded? Mentally ill? Had I ever heard of it?

I couldn't say that I had, but nevertheless, a small spark of hope sprang up. Perhaps this was it. This was no seven day wonder. The announcer had said that it could take months or even years of therapy, but that these children who seemed so much like Drew could be helped. Could this be the key to the mystery of Drew's behavior? It intrigued me enough to stay on my mind the rest of the day.

By the time Gene arrived home from his fishing trip that evening, I was a coiled spring. The children were already in bed, and when I heard his key in the lock, I fairly sprinted across the living room to the front door. "I thought you'd never get home," I said as I pulled him toward the kitchen.

"Whoa, now," Gene said. "Slow down. What's the story here?" His forehead wrinkled as he looked at me. "You all right? The kids ok?"

"Yes, sure. The kids are fine, I'm fine. I'm just--excited, I guess. Or nervous. I don't know."

He seated himself at the table with a glass of tea while I served dinner. I shook so that I nearly dropped the bowl of corn I held. Gene grabbed my hand. "Slow down, will you? I don't have to eat this minute. Why don't you just sit down here and tell me what's going on?"

I took a deep breath and sat on the chair next to him. I clasped my hands together to still the tremor in them. "I think I know what's wrong with Drew," I burst out. I saw a flicker of irritation in Gene's eyes, and wished I could call back my hasty words. I wanted so much to deliver the information in a calm and assured manner so he wouldn't reject it out of hand. From the look on his face, I'd blown it.

He rubbed a hand across his face, then looked at me. "Haven't you had enough of this? There's nothing wrong with Drew."

"But there is, I know there is."

"Look. You took him to Dr. Helmann. He says the kid's all right. Then you took him to that hearing specialist. He says the kid's all right. When are you going to give up?" He leaned back in his chair and shook his head. "Drew's probably the healthiest child we have."

"Then why won't he talk? He's almost three years old and his vocabulary consists of exactly five words." I ticked them off on my fingers: "Sissy, TV Guide, cookie...."

"He can count," Gene pointed out.

"That's just recitation. He learned that when I was teaching John his numbers."

"Well, if he learned that, then he can't be retarded or anything." Gene drained the tea from his glass and went to the refrigerator to pour another.

I turned so I could see him. "I didn't say he's retarded. You haven't even given me a chance to tell you what I think."

He turned from the refrigerator and started back toward the table, a look of exasperation on his face. He seated himself again and set the glass down perhaps a little harder than he had to. He served himself from the platter of fried chicken and spoke without looking at me. "Will you just give it up?"

"No. I won't give up. I won't give up until I see Drew do all the things John and Marie did. I won't give up until I see that he's got the same chance any other child has. I can't believe you don't--"

He sighed. "All right, Julia. Lay it on me. What's wrong with him this week?"

I let the dig pass while I outlined the program I had seen. "And the kids looked and acted just like Drew," I finished.

"Autism? You just said he wasn't retarded."

"I don't think it's the same thing," I said, uncertain now of just what I did think. I pushed my clean plate away and lit a cigarette to borrow time. As I went to the counter for an ashtray, I picked up the paper bag upon which I'd written the phone number given on "Medix." Back at the table, I laid the bag beside Gene's plate. "This is the number they gave on that show. Do you think I ought to call it?"

He reached for another piece of chicken and a second helping of scalloped potatoes. "You do what you think's best, Julia. But don't be too surprised if they laugh you off the line when you tell them your three-year-old doesn't talk much, doesn't like strangers, and acts weird." He laughed himself then. "I mean, what three-year-old doesn't act weird? Remember when John tossed the pennies into Drew's mouth and Drew swallowed them? That's pretty weird on John's part, if you ask me, but I don't see you running around trying to find out what's wrong with him."

I didn't answer. I knew all I had to go on was a vague cluster of behaviors, but I was convinced. Something was wrong with my child, and I meant to find out what it was and how to remedy it, no matter how long it took.

For the next few days, I watched Drew more closely than ever. Maybe Gene was right, and I was wrong. I couldn't say with absolute certainty that Drew was autistic, and I was afraid to call this Dr. Schreibman, afraid that Gene was right and I would make a fool of myself. My last attempt to find a cause for Drew's odd behavior had taken place five months ago, and I wasn't sure I wanted a repeat of it.

. . .

Dr. Helmann's eyes had bored into mine. "Julia, it's not this child who has the problem. It's you."

"But I know something is wrong." I looked at Drew where he squatted in the corner of Dr. Helmann's office. He stood a Frisbee on end, and spun it over and over again. At home, I would have attempted to distract him with another activity. The strange rituals he often performed baffled and even irritated me, and I always tried to halt them. "Look at him, doctor. Is that normal?"

Dr. Helmann cast a brief glance at Drew, then came around the large oak desk and perched on the edge of

it. He took my cold hand in both of his warm ones.
"What will it take to convince you that there's nothing
wrong with that boy?" he asked. His eyes softened, and
I took a deep breath.

"A specialist. You can refer me."

He dropped my hand and threw his own up in the
air. "All right. Fine. A specialist it is." He went around
his desk and pushed the button on the intercom.
"Debbie? Call Jim Talbot over at Otology Associates
and set up an appointment for Julia and Drew Crowder." He released the button and looked at me. "There
now. Are you satisfied?"

My face flamed but I nodded.

Now, as I recalled the scene, the heat rose in my
face again. I grew even warmer as I remembered our
appointment with the specialist to whom Dr. Helmann
had referred us.

. . .

The visit to Otology Associates reinforced my
already negative opinion of the medical profession. Dr.
Talbot had no doubt been apprised of my over
anxiousness by Dr. Helmann. After a brief attempt to
test Drew's hearing, we met in Talbot's office.

He leaned back in his leather chair and smoothed
back his already perfect hair. I gritted my teeth as I
waited for him to speak, sure that if he referred one
more time to my "layman's assumption" of a hearing
impairment, I would scream.

Finally, he spoke, choosing his words as if they were
priceless jewels. "Mrs. Crowder, the problem here is not
with this child's hearing."

I sat up straighter, Drew on my lap. "Then what is it?"

Talbot swiveled in his chair and looked out the window that filled one wall, then sighed and turned back to me. "It's you. You've got to just let him be a child. He doesn't have to operate on some sort of schedule, a developmental time table."

"I don't--"

He waved his hand. "Oh, I know. You modern mothers like to go strictly by the book. If a child is one day over the maximum age for toilet training, you go haywire."

"I've never--I think when a child is almost three and still doesn't talk there's a--"

He stood, seeming to warm to his subject now. "I don't mind telling you, Benjamin Spock has done more harm than--"

Shaking with suppressed rage, I stood and grabbed my purse. "I don't need a dissertation on child rearing," I said, and went to the door with Drew on my hip. When I reached it, I jerked it open and turned to face the doctor. "And I don't read Dr. Spock," I added, and slammed the door behind me.

. . .

Now, on this cloudless California day, I wished that Dr. Spock could give me the answer. I had prayed over and over that I was wrong, that Drew was just a little slow, but my heart knew better. Still, some form of denial still resided within me. I felt that I would do anything to help Drew, but some tiny part of me hesitated to call the number I had seen on television. The paper sack with the number still laid where I had placed it, and I couldn't summon the courage to call.

About five days after the program had aired, I woke up with a sore throat and fever. I got Marie off to school and asked Marilyn to keep John for the day. There was no question of sending Drew to Marilyn's, so I kept him with me. I shut the bedroom door and crawled back into bed. Drew climbed up beside me. I turned on the portable TV by the bed and fell back against the pillows. "Sesame Street" was on, but Drew's gaze, though directed toward the television screen, remained expressionless.

I turned my head toward the phone on the night-stand. By now, the number from the "Medix" program seemed etched on my brain. I couldn't forget it if I wanted to. I looked over at Drew, who leaned against the headboard, eyes fixed on a point near the television, and ran his thumb over the edge of a deck of cards, time after time.

I covered his small hand with mine, and he ceased to stroke the deck. When I removed my hand, he began the motion again. His expression never changed.

I took the cards from him. He didn't look at me, but continued to hold his hand as if the cards were still there. "Come on, lay down with Mommy," I said. He made no sign that he had heard me, and I thought back to what the narrator had said on the "Medix" program, about autistic children giving the appearance of having a hearing impairment, and how they sat for long periods of time engaged in repetitive activity. I sighed and slid down further in the bed. I pulled Drew down beside me and settled him in the crook of my arm. While I admired the sweep of his lashes and his smooth skin, he stared at a spot on the ceiling with expressionless eyes.

"It's just you and me, huh, Drew?" I said. I put my chin on top of his head and felt unshed tears burn my eyes. "I just can't let you live your life this way," I whispered. "I don't care what people think. I'll get help for you somehow."

Just before I dozed off, I felt a vibration begin in Drew's small body as he began a tuneless but eerily beautiful hum.

. . .

I jerked awake and looked at the clock. It was nearly noon. It isn't like Drew to be still so long, I thought, and felt behind me on the bed. He wasn't there. I turned over so quickly it made me dizzy. He wasn't on the bed, and I soon found that he wasn't in the room at all.

I swung my legs over the edge of the bed and stood. The room danced a crazy jig and I grabbed the bedside table to steady myself. "Drew?" I called, surprised at how weak my voice sounded. I made my slow way into the kitchen.

I found no sign of him in the kitchen, nor in the living room. A draft around my ankles made me shiver as I went through the living room and down the hallway. In the boys bedroom I saw only toys and clothes scattered about, the normal clutter of a kid's room. I clutched the edge of the top bunk and fought a wave of dizziness. When my eyes focused once more, I glanced through the window over the bunk bed, the one that looked out on busy Lindley Street. There, just over the center line, stood Drew.

Chapter 2

My breath caught in my throat and hung there. I tried to scream but the words wouldn't come. Another wave of dizziness, this time accompanied by nausea, swept over me. I nearly fell when I turned loose of the bed's metal frame, but I continued on toward the doorway, then into the hall.

"Drew Drew Drew Drew," I chanted, as if that would keep him safe until I could get to him. As I wove my way into the living room a slight gust of air again wafted over me and I saw now what I had not earlier--the front door stood an inch or two ajar.

I lunged toward it and nearly fell again, but somehow I got out the door and into the yard. Drew had made it to the other side of the street and now struggled to get up on the high curb. Unable to mount it standing upright, he grasped it with both hands and tried to lift one leg up onto it. His little legs still fell short and he stood, as if uncertain for a few seconds, then turned and looked at a spot near me.

Terrified that he would try to cross against the heavy noonday traffic, I called to him and struggled to keep my voice even. "Drew, stay right there. Mommy's coming." He didn't look toward me, but kept his eyes averted. My cotton gown flapped around my thighs as I moved on weak legs to the street, but I was only vaguely aware of the curious stares of passing drivers.

I waited for a break in traffic, but there seemed to be no end to the stream of cars. Suddenly, Drew took a step away from the curb, then another, and I could wait no longer. I lunged in front of a compact car, which swerved to miss me and instead, forced a motorcyclist up someone's driveway and across their lawn.

I grabbed Drew and we both tumbled onto the curb and the patch of grass that abutted it. As we hit the ground, I felt my ankle turn with a painful "pop," but I didn't care. All that mattered was that I now held Drew, safe and unharmed.

"Je-sus Chee-rrist, lady! What are you, some kinda fruitcake? What the hell's the matter with you?" The gray-faced driver of the compact car stood over me and glared as he wiped sweat from his face.

"I'm sorry," I said, and stood up, with Drew firmly on my hip. "I just--I was asleep, and he wandered off."

"Well, you was lucky this time," he grumbled. "Been anybody else and they prob'ly woulda run over you. Jesus Christ!" he repeated, and stalked back to his car.

Drew made no sound as I hobbled back across the street. "You scared me spitless," I told him, as we entered the house. "You know you can't go outside without Mommy." I stood him on his feet inside the door, then locked it and slipped the security chain in place.

He headed for the kitchen. "Eh. Eh-h," he began, and I sighed, then followed him.

As I fixed his lunch, the sight of him in the middle of Lindley Street flashed through my mind over and over again, and I felt sick each time. "What if I hadn't woke up?" I asked myself. "What if I'd taken cough syrup, or an antihistamine, and just not woke up until--" I stopped. I couldn't even say the words. I only knew that something had to change. The more mobile he became, the more of a danger Drew was to himself, and I could no longer afford the luxury of thinking I could take proper care of him. Someone, somewhere, knew what was wrong with Drew, and how to fix it. It was up to me to find out where the answer lay.

I put his lunch on a tray and led him back into the bedroom. Though I knew the front door was locked and chained, I took no chances. I stuck a heavy metal letter opener into the wood between the frame and the door's trim, with the handle protruding over the door, making an effective door stop.

I lay in bed beside Drew, and watched him pick cheese- covered macaroni up one at a time and place them on his spoon, which he then placed in his mouth.

I turned onto my other side and looked at the phone. Dr. Schreibman's name ricocheted through my mind, followed by the phone number I had heard on "Medix." I looked at the phone again. Maybe Gene was right. Maybe she would laugh me off the line.

I looked at Drew, who averted his eyes and picked up a piece of macaroni. I looked back at the phone, and suddenly, I made up my mind. Maybe this Dr. Schreibman would laugh at me. Maybe she'd tell me not to waste my time trying to find someone who would agree that there was something wrong with Drew. Then again, maybe she wouldn't.

I sat up on the edge of the bed and dialed the phone number that ran through my head. I uttered a quick prayer and, for good measure, crossed my fingers as I waited for the ringing to be answered.

Chapter 3

When Dr. Laurie Schreibman came on the line, she sounded impossibly young, and I said so. She laughed, a musical sound that made me want to laugh too, but I was too nervous.

"I-I saw the 'Medix' program the other day."

"Oh?" Laughter turned to interest.

"Yes. My son--he just looks a lot like those kids. And they said on there that autism is often mistaken for a hearing impairment."

"It is. Mrs. Crowder, tell me a little bit about your son."

"Well, he just turned three." I thought of all the little things I had noticed in Drew, and didn't quite know where to start. I sat silently for several moments, then Dr. Schreibman prompted me.

"How about his relationships with others?"

"He really doesn't relate to anybody but me, and that's only been in the last year or year and a half. Unless people approach him, it's as if they don't exist. In the grocery store, if someone comes up and tries to talk to him, his eyes just get--well, his whole face looks like a storm cloud. And he never, ever looks you in the eye. He'll break his neck to avoid making eye contact."

"Does he play with other children?"

"No. Not even his brother. And if people come to the house, he just sort of fades away, and when I go to look for him, I usually find him asleep in a closet."

"How about his language?"

"What language?" I asked. He's three years old, and he only says four or five words." I heard the rate of her breathing change. "Besides that, it's as if he doesn't understand me when I talk, either. Sometimes he seems to, but usually I get no response at all. He's only three, and already I-I can't control him. I haven't been to church in a year, because I can't keep him from running all over the place and disrupting the service. Shopping for groceries is an ordeal unless I have someone along to help me with him."

I looked at Drew where he sat on the bed, still eating macaroni a piece at a time. "Most things I notice are just--really subtle. When I've tried to talk to his pediatrician about it, he just laughs, and says I'm an over-anxious mother."

"How about--does he ever rock for long periods of time? For instance, would he continue to rock for hours if you didn't stop him?"

"Well," I said slowly, "He doesn't rock, but he does do--funny things. He acts funny."

"In what way, Mrs. Crowder?" Her interest seemed to be increasing, but without the skepticism I normally heard.

"Take this morning, for instance. He sat right here beside me and stared into space, and ran his thumb over the edge of a deck of cards. Just that, over and over. I usually stop him, because it's so strange, but he'll go on and on with it if I don't."

"He's self-stimming," she said, almost to herself.

"What?"

"Self-stimulating behavior. Kind of rituals that autistic kids are inclined to do. Is there anything else?"

I thought for a moment, then said, "Sometimes he just runs. He goes from a specific spot in the kitchen to a specific spot in the hall over and over till he's exhausted. And he eats all the time. He eats three or four bowls of cereal in the morning, and it has to have raisins in it--he doesn't just want raisins in it, he has to have raisins in it. He chews everything thirty or forty times--when I'm fixing lunch, Drew is still eating breakfast."

"Mrs. Crowder, I want you to start at the beginning, all right? When did you first notice that there was something wrong with Drew?"

I took a trembling breath. Finally, someone would listen to me! Ever since I first suspected a problem with Drew, a thought had imbedded itself in my mind, that if I didn't find help for him by the time he was three, he might never catch up. This could be the person that would tell me what was wrong with Drew, that would help me to help him.

As Dr. Schreibman listened, the words tumbled out of me. I couldn't speak quickly enough. Sentences ran together, words fought for dominance over each other, and I talked until I was hoarse. When I finished, Dr. Schreibman seemed to breath a sigh of relief with me. I was sure she must think I was some kind of a nut case. I felt near tears at the rejection I knew was coming.

Instead, she seemed even more interested. "What about now? Didn't you say he still won't relate to strangers?"

"Right. When people come up to him in the grocery store or somewhere, his little face bunches up like a fist. He just acts like he hates them, like they're invading his world, and he doesn't like it one bit."

There was only silence for a moment, then I heard the doctor exhale. "Mrs. Crowder, I want to set up an appointment for you with Dr. Lovaas. He's head of the Young Autism Project at UCLA. I think maybe we can help your son."

Chapter 4

After I talked to Dr. Schreibman, I felt a sort of electricity go through my body. Every nerve seemed to stand at attention, and, though still unwell, I found that I could not stay down. I crawled back into bed with Drew several times, my aching head and body demanding rest, only to crawl out again within minutes.

I paced back and forth through the house in my nightgown and tried to imagine what this autism thing was all about. Try as I might, I could not remember ever having heard the term before I saw the "Medix" show.

After I paced and smoked for an hour or so, I decided to get dressed and go next door to get John. I might as well bring him home if I'm not going to rest, I thought as I pulled on a pair of slacks and a blouse, and dragged a comb through my tangled hair. Slipping into my shoes, I hefted Drew onto my hip and went next door.

By the time I made it the short distance, I found it difficult to breath, and perspiration trickled down my back in spite of the mild temperature. Drew bounced on my hip, taking the little jaunt as he did everything--void of emotion and silent.

When no one answered my knock, I pushed the door open and went in. "Marilyn? It's Julia. Where are you?" I heard a racket from the rear of the house and John ran toward me.

His disheveled hair and sparkling dark eyes told me that he was having a terrific time. "Mommy, we're makin' you a s'prise only I can't tell you it's a ashtray!" he shouted, then clapped his hands over his mouth. His eyes grew huge, and I thought he was going to cry. "I said it--I told about the s'prise."

I squatted beside him and gave him a hug. "Oh, Honey, that's all right. Mommy's got an ear ache--I didn't hear a thing you said."

He grinned at me and I ruffled his hair, then watched him race off shouting for Marilyn. "My mommy's here. She don't know about the s'prise 'cause she gots a ear ache," he screamed. His words bounced off the walls and my head pounded in response.

I raised myself to a standing position with Drew still astride my hip. I couldn't help but compare his passivity to John's boundless energy and enthusiasm.

Marilyn came out of her combination studio-office in a paint-stained smock with a scarf over her hair.

"Hi," she said. "I thought I'd get a couple of pots fired since I got the kiln fixed." She smoothed her blondish bangs back from her forehead, and they flopped right back where they had been. "I guess John told you he was making you something?"

I nodded. "Of course. I didn't hear a thing, though, what with my ear ache and all."

"Right," she said, as she grinned and brushed her bangs back again. "I'll bet they heard him in the next county, though." She gave me an appraising glance and shook her head. "You look like hell," she said. "Did you get any rest at all?" She moved a stack of folded clothing from the couch to the coffee table and motioned for me to sit down. "Do you feel like a glass of tea, or some coffee?"

I lowered myself onto the couch, sure the creaking of my bones would be audible. "Coffee would be nice," I said, and sat Drew beside me. He hummed to himself and watched intently as he splayed his fingers, then curled them into his palm again and again. Normally, I would have tried to stop him, but Dr. Schreibman's comment that Drew's odd behavior could be a part of something bigger, something that could be treated, cast a different light on his action. I found myself almost fearful that the behavior would disappear before our appointment with this Dr. Lovaas, and we would be consigned again to the limbo of the unknown. I wasn't sure I could stand that.

"Julia?" I started at the sound of Marilyn's voice, and saw her in front of me with a mug in her hand and a look of concern on her face. "Are you okay?"

I took the mug from her and tried to smile, but couldn't quite pull it off. "I'm fine. I guess I was day dreaming."

She sat down across from me in a corduroy recliner. "You seem so--I don't know--distracted, I guess. And tired."

I sighed. "I still don't feel very well, but I just couldn't stay down." I hesitated for a moment, then asked, "Have you ever heard of something called 'autism?'" The hand in which I held the mug of coffee trembled so much that I had to use my other one to steady it.

Marilyn's eyes narrowed, and she blew upward at her bangs, then brushed them off her forehead with her hand. "Artesian? Like an artesian well?"

I shook my head. "No. 'Autism.' A-u-t-i-s-m, I think. Something like that."

She pursed her lips for a moment and frowned. "Isn't that kind of like, retarded or something? Seems like I read an article about it somewhere. Little kids get it, I think."

"Retarded? No, I don't think so. That can't be it." My head spun from the combination of nervous energy and illness, and this information did not help.

Marilyn looked at me. "Julia, you look awful. Here, let me take that--" She reached for my cup, and got it just before I would have spilled it all over the carpet, couch, and coffee table.

I stood on wobbly legs. "I think I should have stayed in bed," I said. I tried to pick Drew up, but couldn't manage it. Instead, I stood him on his feet and took his hand. "I think I'll go back over and lie down," I told Marilyn, my voice weak. "Maybe John had better stay here until Gene gets home, if it's okay with you." I made a wobbly line for the door and Marilyn followed me.

"Sure," she said, and patted my shoulder as I opened the front door. As I walked across the lawn between our houses with Drew on my hip, she called to me. "Are you sure everything is all right, Julia?"

I waved her back. "Fine. Everything's fine," I said, but I wasn't sure of that at all. I hurried into the house, and pulled Drew with me. I heard him begin a whine deep in his throat. "Oh, God, Drew. You can't be hungry again already." I looked at the clock. It was barely two hours since he'd eaten, but I knew I'd do nearly anything to stave off the screeching soon to come.

I poured some dry cereal in a bowl for him, then hauled him and the bowl back to the bedroom. As I started to lower myself on the bed beside Drew, inspiration seized me and I dragged myself to the living room where I dug through the book case until I found what I was looking for.

"Ah ha!" I said, and pulled out a worn dictionary. I flipped through the tissue-thin pages until I found the word I was looking for. "'Autism,'" I read. "Psychol. A state of mind characterized by daydreaming, hallucinations, and disregard of external reality."

My mind latched on to only one word in the whole of the definition--hallucination. People who had hallucinations were mentally ill. I knew that much. How could a little child be mentally ill? I wondered, then thought of Marilyn's offering. Retarded. Which was it? Retarded, or mentally ill? If these were the choices confronting us, what good would a diagnosis be? The nervous energy present an hour before now turned to panic. I sank into a nearby chair. I felt almost sorry that I had called Dr. Schreibman. Maybe knowing what was wrong with Drew would be worse than not knowing, after all.

. . .

When I told Gene about my conversation with Dr. Schreibman, he shook his head, a half-smile on his face, as if to say, "Well, folks, here she goes again--another wild goose chase."

"Julia, when are you going to give up?"

"When Drew has the same chance in life anybody else does."

"For God's sake, don't be so melodramatic. There's nothing wrong with Drew that time won't cure if you'll quit dragging him all over hell and creation looking for a problem."

Stung, I stalked out onto the patio and lit a cigarette. Gene was wrong. I knew he was. In three years, Drew had only gotten worse. His behavior became more bizarre and he became more uncontrollable. "Time will not cure this," I muttered.

That evening, I went into the boys' bedroom. "Hi, guys," I said. "Time to wind down and get to bed. Let's pick out a bedtime story, ok?"

John left his crayons and coloring book and went to the small white bookcase in the corner. He brought back a tattered book. "Green Eggs and Ham, ok? Let's read that."

John came to where Drew and I sat in the oversized rocker in one corner of the bedroom. "Scoot over," he said. "Let me sit here, too." He wedged his sturdy body in between Drew and I, then beamed up at me. "I like to sit here."

"I see that," I said, and glanced at Drew. While John approached our evening ritual with energy and excitement, Drew only seemed to tolerate it, as he did everything.

When we had finished the Dr. Seuss classic, I carried Drew to the bottom bunk and laid him down. As I bent to kiss him good-night, John wiggled up from the foot of the bed to get between Drew and me.

"What are you doing?" I asked. "Get up there on your bed, and I'll be up there in a minute."

He grinned and wiggled back down to the end of the bed and onto the floor. "I want Drew's kiss, too," he said, and giggled as he climbed up the ladder to his bed.

I bent over Drew, and wiggled my forefinger in ever-smaller circles over his stomach. "Busy Bee's going to get you," I said, and circled my finger closer and closer to his stomach. Suddenly, I felt some movement in my hair and jerked my head around. John hung over the top bunk, a huge grin on his face.

He held up one finger. "Busy Bee's getting in your hair," he said. He giggled and drew his head back up, out of view.

I sighed and shook my head. John seemed to be everywhere at times. I turned my attention back to Drew. "Mommy loves you," I said, and kissed him on the cheek. "Night-night." I stood and looked at John where he lay on the top bunk, wriggling in anticipation of his nightly tickle. I circled my finger over his belly and, before I even came close, he doubled up in giggles, then threw his arms around my neck. "Busy Bee makes me laugh even when he don't touch me, Mommy."

I laughed, and hugged him back, proud of the life and vitality he brought to everything. Still, I couldn't help comparing him to Drew. I didn't begrudge John his vitality, but I wished that Drew could have just a tenth as much. Life might sometimes be painful for John, but how much worse must it be to feel nothing but occasional anger, as Drew seemed to.

I turned out the light and stood in the doorway a moment. "Just heal him, Lord," I prayed. "I'll take a straight-out, unexplainable miracle, or I'll take it through people. But you've just got to heal him."

. . .

On the morning of the appointment at UCLA, I set off with both boys in the back seat, and a mixture of fear and hope in my heart. I could hear John as he bounced around in the back seat and chattered to his silent brother. "I'm Captain Kirk, Drew. You be Mr. Spock." He made a series of weird whirring and beeping noises. "See all them cars? Klingons! Help! Scotty! Beam me up, Scotty."

I glanced in the rear-view mirror to where Drew sat in his battered car seat, straight and silent, eyes expressionless. My heart ached for both boys--John, forced to play all parts in any game, and Drew, locked in his own private suit of armor.

As I accelerated to merge with the freeway traffic, John's voice changed. "Leave the door alone. Mommy, Drew's out of his car seat again. He keeps on messing with the door handle." I saw John bounce across the back seat, and heard the click of the door lock as he slapped it down. I heard another click as Drew must have immediately pulled the door handle up. "Mommy, Drew keeps on--"

"Ok, ok, ok," I said, and pulled over onto the shoulder of the road. I turned around on my knees, and tried to push Drew down into his car seat. The old seat was a mess--the strap meant to fasten between the child's legs was long gone, and foam poked through the cracked black vinyl. Drew had done most of the damage in earlier efforts to escape its restraint.

Drew's knees locked as he resisted me, and I finally had to forcibly bend them to get him to sit. I pushed down the padded guard around the car seat, and wished for the hundredth time that we could afford a new one.

Driving on the freeway was frightening enough without worrying about Drew opening a door and falling out of the car.

"John, try to keep him from getting out, all right? Hold this thing--" I laid my hand on the guard, "--down and see if you can keep him in."

I had barely merged with the other traffic before I heard John. "Mommy, he won't stay in. He acts like Jello. He just slides out the bottom."

I heard a click as the back door was unlocked again, and swerved to the side of the road. As soon as I stopped the car, I turned around and hauled Drew into the front seat with me. "Come on, John. You, too." With one arm tightly around Drew's chest and John holding his feet, we arrived at UCLA only a few minutes late.

Dr. O. Ivar Lovaas presented a picture much different than I expected. Instead of a small, pipe-smoking, goateed man, he stood tall, clean-shaven, and energetic, intelligence and friendliness apparent in his face and demeanor.

As he introduced himself, he took one of my hands in both his and squeezed. "This has been very hard on you, has it not?" he asked, with just a hint of an accent.

I didn't know if he meant the trip from home this morning, or the past three years, but my raw nerves responded at once to the sympathy in his voice, and I intuitively felt that he understood what a long hard road it had been. He motioned to a folding table across the room. A woman sat in a metal chair, and a man perched on the edge of the table. "These are my assistants--Doug, and Paula." He smiled at me. "They are graduate students--psychology majors."

I nodded to both, and Dr. Lovaas led me to another chair at the table. John followed, but Drew turned and went to the door. On tiptoe, he tried to grasp the knob with both hands. "Eh-h, eh, eh," he whined. I started after him, but Dr. Lovaas got there first. He grasped Drew beneath the arms and carried him over to one corner where toys overflowed from a large wooden box. Turning, he motioned to John. "Come on, Son. You may play, also." He stood Drew on his feet, but retained a hold on him, and pulled several toys out for the child's inspection while Drew continued his familiar whine, face averted from Dr. Lovaas.

John stood beside the toy box, silent at first. After a moment, he pulled on Dr. Lovaas' trouser leg. "Drew likes that," he said, and pointed to something in the toy box.

Dr. Lovaas pulled a Jack-in-the-box out and put it in front of Drew's face. "Do you want to play with this, Drew?"

Drew's whining ceased and he grabbed the toy. He squatted and set it on the floor, pushed the lid down so the clown disappeared from view, and began to turn the handle. John watched his brother for a moment, then dug into the box himself.

Dr. Lovaas came back to the table and seated himself. He patted my hand. "They will be fine," he said, as if he read my mind. "Tell me, Mrs. Crowder, when was it you first noticed something different about Drew?"

With that, we launched into a two-hour interview. Paula sat across from me at the table and scribbled furiously as I told Dr. Lovaas of all the worry, the fruitless questioning of doctors, my attempts to have Drew's hearing tested, and many other things I had not remembered when I talked with Dr. Schreibman. As I wound down, I looked at Dr. Lovaas. "And now, I keep hearing the term 'autism.' Drew does act like the kids I saw on Medix, but how do I know this isn't another blind alley?" When I finished, exhausted and breathless, I lit a cigarette and shifted in my seat as I waited for him to speak.

Dr. Lovaas sat very still and watched the smoke from my cigarette as it wafted toward the ceiling. Finally, he said, "Autism is a puzzling disorder. Many children who are eventually diagnosed as being autistic may first be thought hearing impaired because of their lack of responsiveness. However, other signs must also be present." Apparently warming to his subject, he rose and stood in the center of the room, as of lecturing a class. He gestured as he ticked off the criteria for autism.

"The child may not speak, or, if he does, it may be simply repetition. He may repel any physical contact, even with mother. He avoids eye contact. He may rock his body forth and back for long periods of time, or stare at an object, such as a fan. He insists on sameness, always sameness. His food must be the same, his routine must never vary. These are behaviors you have described to me, are they not, Mrs. Crowder?"

Dazed, I nodded, and watched Drew push the clown into its box, then crank the handle.

Dr. Lovaas flashed me a toothy grin and rubbed his hands together. "G-o-o-o-d," he said, stringing the word out in a breathy burst of enthusiasm.

I saw Drew jerk his head sharply up at the strange-sounding word. Maybe Dr. Lovaas was right, and Drew only appeared to be hearing impaired. He certainly seemed to hear some sounds.

"Now," Dr. Lovaas said, "There are some criteria that must be met in order for Drew to be admitted to the Young Autism program." He smiled at me. "One, both you and your husband must agree to take part in the therapy sessions. You will work directly with your son. The schedule will be exhausting, hours each day, every day of the week. Two, you must place John in day care in order to give yourself free time to work with Drew, and also for John's own sake." He looked at me. "Agreed?"

I looked at John. He played with the unfamiliar toys, completely engrossed in them. Drew sat in silence with the Jack-in-the-box, pushing the clown from view and turning the crank until it popped up again, over and over. I didn't know where the money would come from to put John in daycare. I didn't know where the time and energy would come from to work long hours with Drew. Nevertheless, I nodded my head in assent. I would do anything, pay any price, if it mean my son could have a life like any other child.

I thought Dr. Lovaas had finished, but he had one final item. My heart sank as I heard the words. "Three. We must have a referral from a doctor independent of the Young Autism Project."

Chapter 5

On the day of our appointment with Dr. J.Q. Simmons, we arrived a few minutes early. In the waiting room, Drew immediately tried to go back out the door, a nasal whine beginning in his throat. I picked him up and took him back to the chair where I had been sitting. It took all my strength to keep him on my lap.

"Eh-h, ehh, eh-h-h," he whined, the whine rapidly escalating to a shriek.

"Sh-h," I said into his ear. I kept a firm hold on him, but I knew it was only a matter of minutes before he was out of my arms.

Instead of becoming quieter, Drew seemed to become more determined. His shrieks took on an angry quality and he kicked his legs.

I winced as his feet whacked into my shins again and again. We were alone in the waiting room except for Dr. Simmons' receptionist. She glanced at us as Drew shrieked, and I felt the heat rise in my face.

"I'm sorry," I said. "He just--doesn't like to be restrained."

"Would it help if you were in a smaller room, with no one else there?" she asked.

"It might," I gasped as Drew struggled. "I'll try anything." I followed her down a narrow hallway and into a room devoid of all furniture except for one upholstered chair. Some stuffed animals and spongy balls laid in a corner.

As soon as the door closed behind us, I released Drew and sank into the chair. The more controls I put on him, the worse he gets, I thought. "If he's even accepted into this Young Autism Project, how will we ever survive?" I wondered as he ran to the door and stood on tiptoe trying to reach the higher-than-normal knob. He still shrieked, but the intensity of it diminished when the receptionist left us.

Finally, when Drew saw that he couldn't reach the door knob, he gradually quieted down. After a few minutes, he leaned back against the door and slid to a sitting position. He held one hand in front of his face, fingers extended, and closed the hand one finger at a time. He stared at it and continued the movement for another ten minutes or so. A knock sounded at the door then, and I picked up Drew and placed him on my hip. He still waved his fingers, but I grabbed his hand in mine as the door opened a little, and the receptionist stuck her head in.

"Dr. Simmons will see you now," she said.

I followed her back down the hall and into a small office, almost completely filled by a large desk. A gray-haired man rose from a swivel chair behind the desk and extended his hand toward me.

"Mrs. Crowder. Won't you sit down?" He motioned to a straight-backed chair to one side of the massive desk.

I seated myself and attempted to hold Drew on my lap, but he struggled so violently I let him go. He ran to the door and tried to turn the knob with both hands, to no avail. I started to rise but Dr. Simmons waved me back.

"He's fine," Dr. Simmons said just as Drew started his familiar droning whine. The doctor bent over and slid a sturdy yellow truck from beneath his desk toward Drew. "I keep this for just such emergencies," he smiled.

The truck rolled across the wood floor and came to a rest after barely brushing Drew's heels. Drew stopped whining and looked down at the truck. He seemed to find it to his liking, because he dropped to his knees, turned it upside down and began spinning one of the black plastic wheels.

Dr. Simmons seemed to want to know many of the same things Dr. Lovaas had: When did I first notice Drew's strange behavior? How did he relate to other people? Did he talk, and if so, how much? At that point, I explained my long-held theory that Drew was hearing impaired. "Only it's a funny kind of impairment," I said. "It's like he can't hear big noises, but the small ones will get his attention."

Apparently a man of action, Dr. Simmons picked up a stack of books from the edge of his desk, raised them above his head, and let them crash to the floor. True to form, Drew didn't respond, but continued to spin the truck's wheel.

Dr. Simmons pursed his lips for a moment and studied Drew, then made a soft quacking sound, reminiscent of Donald Duck. I could see Drew's spine stiffen, and he turned to stare at the doctor. With a lopsided grin, he let go of the truck, rose, and walked over to Dr. Simmons. He placed his small hand on the man's arm and stared at him. Dr. Simmons quacked, and Drew grinned once more.

"Drew, you're a good looking little boy. How are you?" Drew's smile disappeared. He turned his back on the doctor and marched back to the truck, where he resumed spinning the wheel.

I sighed, and looked at Dr. Simmons. "See what I mean?"

"Hmm. Yes." He leaned back in his chair. "How about your own health?" he asked.

"Excuse me?" The question seemed somewhat out of context.

"After Drew was born. Did you have any illnesses that, perhaps, took you away from him when he was an infant?"

"No. I mean, I did become very ill, when Drew was about four or five months old, but I wasn't away from him. On the contrary, I spent more time holding and playing with him than with either of my other two children, because I was bedridden for a while."

Dr. Simmons leaned forward and clasped his hands together on the desk. "I see. What was the problem?"

"I have systemic lupus," I told him. "That was the first episode. I couldn't walk for about three weeks, because of the pain and swelling in my ankles, and I kept Drew right beside me all the time. Even after I was back on my feet, I could only be up for about twenty minutes before I had to sit down and elevate my feet for another twenty minutes, so I held him a lot then, too."

Dr. Simmons eyes narrowed slightly. "What about medication?"

"Oh. I had almost forgotten about that. The doctor put me on 60 grains of aspirin a day--I had to stop breast feeding Drew then, and put him on formula. We were really worried about that, because John had had an intolerance to--" A thought struck me, and I felt the blood drain from my face. "You don't suppose--I couldn't have caused whatever's wrong with Drew, could I, Doctor?"

He leaned back in his chair and placed his finger tips together. "Well, I rather doubt it. But there is a theory some people in the field hold--of the 'refrigerator mother.' It refers to a parent who is cold and unresponsive to her child, and this perhaps contributes to the development of autism." He put the tips of his fingers together and moved the chair in small arcs. "I, personally, don't agree with that."

Whether it was his theory or not, I felt weak. Could "refrigerator mother" describe me? I was reserved, yes, and not given to small talk, but I had always been completely open and loving with my children. I knew when I had them what a responsibility I was taking on, and had always felt up to the task. Suddenly, I abandoned that train of thought as the significance of what Dr. Simmons had just said hit me. "Are you saying that Drew is definitely autistic?" I asked, dread and hope battling within me for supremacy.

He shook his head. "I can't give you a definite answer to that question yet," he said. "I'll make my recommendation to Dr. Lovaas in a few days."

He stood and held his hand out to me. Dazed, I shook it, then stood and turned to Drew, who still spun the wheel on the yellow truck. As I picked him up and went to the door, I looked into his eyes and tried to penetrate that wall he had built around himself. He looked away from me, lifted a hand, and began closing it, slowly, one finger at a time, in front of his face.

0   From behind me, I heard Dr. Simmons voice. "Mrs. Crowder?" I turned to look at him.

"If Dr. Lovaas's program is not for your son, we'll find one that is. Try not to worry."

I turned and carried my son out into the warm California sunshine. How can I not worry? I thought. What if it's my fault Drew is this way? How can I ever live with myself? These questions and more spun in my head as we drove home to begin yet another wait.

Chapter 6

The time between the visit with Dr. Simmons and the call from Dr. Lovaas's office seemed interminable. My conviction that Drew must have help by the age of three was stronger than ever, and time was slipping away from us. He turned three on January 5, and it was now the middle of February. When I considered how quickly days became weeks and weeks months, panic almost overtook me.

Gene and I hardly spoke, and when we did, he offered little comfort. "You worry too much," he often said. "These guys are professionals, and if Drew really has a problem, they'll figure out what it is and fix it. It's as simple as that."

Easy for you to say, I thought. You don't think there's anything wrong with him anyway. At times, I wanted to forcibly wipe the smug look from his face, but on the rare occasions when I did display my temper, it frightened the children and left Gene untouched.

More than once, I thought about how much he had wanted children. "Let's have at least five," he had said when we were married.

I wasn't sure I wanted any until I held my firstborn in my arms. I fell hopelessly in love with Marie, and with John and Drew in turn. I had thought we would share the rearing of our family, but it had not turned out that way. The older they got, the more distant their father became. I had hoped finding some sort of help for Drew would draw us closer, but now I wasn't so sure.

Finally, on February 12, 1975, the phone rang. Somehow, I knew it was Dr. Lovaas' office, and before I hung up, I agreed to bring Drew in on February 14. As I cradled the phone, I breathed a sigh of relief and a prayer of hope. "Just let us be on the right track," I whispered.

. . .

I approached the scheduled meeting with some trepidation. I still didn't know what Dr. Simmons' recommendation to Dr. Lovaas had been. Perhaps Dr. Lovaas only asked us in to explain why he couldn't take Drew into the program. He had seemed to be that kind of man, one who would be very careful to make himself understood.

Still, I derived a small amount of comfort from Dr. Simmons's last words to me. "If Dr. Lovaas's program is not for your son, we'll find one that is."

I arranged for John to stay at Marilyn's, and headed for the car with Drew. I put the car seat in front with me, then placed Drew in it. His dark eyes watched me with little expression, but I knew he was intent on what I was doing.

I took an extra-long leather belt from my purse and put it around the back of the car seat and his waist, and buckled it behind the seat. He peered at me for a moment, then tensed his whole body as if trying to loosen the belt. I checked to make sure it was not too tight, then, satisfied, got in the car myself.

At first, Drew strained against the belt, and even tried to slip out of it, but to no avail. I braced myself, ready for an onslaught of whines, shrieks, or both, but after he initially tested the belt's hold, he averted his head from me and stared out the window as he rocked back and forth.

I heaved a sigh of relief, and maneuvered the car onto the freeway. As I drove to UCLA, I wished that Gene were with me now. He had promised that he would be, but I should have known better. He would never accept the fact that he had an imperfect son. Sometimes it seemed that everything came before our children. "Strange behavior for a man who insisted on a big family," I muttered.

I pulled into the parking garage on the UCLA campus and cut the motor. Drew looked around the area with no more interest than if he had been there a dozen times. But as we walked toward Franz Hall, the white stone building that housed Dr. Lovaas' offices, he stopped and gazed at the large fountain. Drops of water caught the California sun and reflected it in a glorious rainbow, and he seemed enchanted.

After a few minutes, I tugged him away from the water and toward the wide brick steps, but he stopped every few seconds to look back at the fountain. We finally made it to the elevator and up to the fifth floor.

As we came through the door, I looked around the huge room with its green and white tile and hordes of toys. Dr. Lovaas gave us a wide, toothy grin, and his handsome Scandinavian face brightened. He stepped over and around a series of expensive-looking video equipment and came toward me.

"Ah, Mrs. Crowder! And how are you this fine day?" he asked, and led us to one of the long folding tables. "And how is Drew?" He squatted down until they were eye to eye. Drew averted his eyes, and gazed at the wall on our left.

I felt comfortable with Dr. Lovaas, even though he was at times more enthusiastic than I was accustomed to men being. I chalked that up to his European background and accepted it gratefully. It was at least a change from Gene's almost emotionless response to Drew's problem. He seated me, then himself at the long table, and leaned across to take both my hands in his.

"We have heard from Dr. Simmons, and he has recommended that we take Drew on the program. He feels, as I do, that Drew is autistic."

I let a slow breath out through my nose, and my body seemed to go limp. Dr. Lovaas looked at me and his eyes widened. "Are you all right? You are very pale--"

To my horror, I had to sniff back tears. "I'm just so relieved. I don't know why--just to know that Drew has a chance, I guess." He handed me a white handkerchief, and I wiped my eyes. "You don't know how it's been. Gene won't talk to me about it, and I don't want to burden my folks." I sniffed. "Sometimes I think I'll go crazy."

"That is understandable," he said as he patted my shoulder. "Caring for children is very stressful. Special children such as Drew are even more so. But, now, we are here to help you."

When I had collected myself, Dr. Lovaas introduced me to a tall, slender young woman with long, dark hair. "This is Andrea Ackerman. She will be working, along with Laurie, Howard, and Martha," he nodded to the

three other people around the table, "as Drew's therapist. She will be the team leader."

Andrea held her hand out to me, and flipped her
hair back over her shoulder. She looks so young--they
all do, I thought as I shook her hand. I resolved to not
let their youth stand in the way of my trust. I already
felt safe with Dr. Lovaas, and if he felt comfortable in
working with these young people, then so would I.

Dr. Lovaas rubbed his hands together. "Are we
ready to go to work?" he asked. I nodded. "Go-o-od,"
he said, and we all laughed at the way Drew's head
jerked up at the sound.

The laughter broke the ice, and Andrea motioned
for me to follow her down a long, narrow hallway. She
carried a sheaf of papers, and some sort of book as she
led me into a small room with only a table, two chairs
and a tape recorder.

"OK, Mrs. Crowder--"

I shook my head. "Please. Just Julia. Every time
I hear 'Mrs. Crowder,' I look for my mother-in-law."

She smiled. "All right. Julia." She tapped the sheaf
of papers in front of her as we seated ourselves. "I'm
going to ask you a number of questions from this test.
It's called the Vineland. There's no need to be nervous,
now, right?"

I smiled at her earnestness. "Right."

"OK. Now. When did Drew first sit up?"

"At about five months," I said.

She made a notation on the paper in front of her.
"At what age did he begin babbling? You know--goo,
goo and ga ga and all that?"

I lit a cigarette and frowned. "Well, actually, he
never did. We used to kind of laugh about it, he was
such a quiet baby."

"I see. When did he say his first word?" She held her pen poised for my answer.

"Right around a year old. But it was the only one he said for a very long time."

"OK. And when did he crawl?"

"Actually, it was after he walked."

Andrea raised her eyebrows. "How's that?"

"Well, he started out, when he was about six months old, scooting around the house on his behind. He got around just fine that way, and he did it until he learned to walk." I tapped the ashes from my cigarette. "My sister, who is in the special education field, told me about some new things in that area. She said that some experts were teaching children who had skipped the crawling stage how to crawl, even though they're already walking--she said they felt that the children who never crawled had missed an important developmental stage." I shrugged, and shifted in my chair. It all sounded so silly now as I explained it to this earnest young woman who probably knew ten times more than I about child-hood development. "So I taught him how to crawl," I finished.

She nodded. "Was it fairly easy to teach him things?"

"Physical things, yes. But anything else, forget it." I hesitated a moment, then said, "Actually, I taught him to walk, too."

"Really? How did that come about?" She made a few more marks on her paper.

"Marie and John both walked early--eight and nine months. When Drew hadn't even tried by ten months,

I decided to teach him. I held onto him while he took steps, and in no time he was doing it on his own."

Andrea pursed her lips and tapped them with her pen. "Did he ever walk on his toes?"

What a strange question, I thought, and shook my head. "I don't remember ever seeing him do that. Why? What does it mean?"

"Well, some professionals believe that small children who walk on their toes may have a chemical imbalance." She shrugged, as if to show that she was not one of "those" professionals.

"Hm," I said.

She shuffled through the papers in front of her for a moment, then looked up at me. "How is his language now? Does he talk much?"

I shook my head. "No. He can say shirt, TV Guide, and cookie. That's about it, I guess." I flipped ashes from my cigarette. "Oh. And Sissy." I laughed as I explained the origin of that particular word. "Marie was six-and-a-half when Drew was born. I don't think she ever forgave me for having another boy, but still, she was thrilled with Drew, and insisted that Sissy be his first word." I tilted my head as I recalled Marie's single-mindedness. "She'd put her nose to his so he had to look at her, and say, 'Sissy. Sissy. Say 'Sissy', Drew.' And finally, he did."

Andrea made a notation, then looked up at me. "OK. I guess that's it for now. You've been very helpful," she said, and grinned. As she stood, she said, "You've really had your hands full, haven't you, Julia?"

A veil of tears rose in front of my eyes. The support, sympathy and understanding I had received in the last few days were almost unbearably precious to me. For the last two or three years, it had been as if Drew and I were marooned on an island of misunderstanding as I tried over and over to explain his behavior to people. Now, suddenly, a rescue boat had come to save us, filled with people willing to not only listen, but to help.

Andrea seemed to know what I was feeling as she came around to me and squeezed my shoulders. "Drew's going to come along beautifully here. I just know it," she said.

As we started out of the room, she stopped. "I forgot," she said, and held out the book she had been carrying. "We'd like you to read this before you return for the next session."

I read the title aloud. "Fundamentals of Behavior Modification." I nodded. "OK. I'll do my best."

When we rejoined Dr. Lovaas and the others, the doctor once again outlined the agreement Gene and I were to make in order to keep Drew in the Young Autism program.

"You will both work with Drew--you must be faithful, attend every session, here and in your home. We will conduct therapy six days a week. And John must go to daycare. Agreed?"

I nodded my head, agreeing for both Gene and I. Andrea handed me a form.

"When you get home, the two of you should fill this out and sign it. Bring it back next time, all right?"

I nodded, folded it and stuck the sheet of paper in my purse. As I did, Dr. Lovaas strode to the toy box. All around it toys lay scattered, and Drew squatted in the midst of them, playing with the Jack-in-the-box.

The doctor took a xylophone from among the toys, and hit several keys with a little mallet. Drew looked up with interest at the pinging sound. "Go-o-ood, Drew," Dr. Lovaas said, then straightened his knees and turned. "Andi, why don't we get some of these toys together and see if Drew will go for toys as reinforcers?"

I watched, mystified, as Andrea, Martha, and Laurie gathered armloads of toys and piled them in the middle of the floor. Dr. Lovaas took a folding chair and seated himself near the toys. By now, Drew had the xylophone, and made tentative "pings" on the keys. Dr. Lovaas reached over and took it from him. I braced myself for Drew's reaction, but it did not come with the intensity I had expected. His eyes narrowed and his whole face tensed, but he made no sound. "Look!" Dr. Lovaas commanded.

Drew ignored the command and began turning the handle of the Jack-in-the-box he had pulled from amid the toys. Dr. Lovaas took the Jack-in-the-box from him and again said, "Look!" in a voice filled with authority.

Drew ignored him and sat with brows drawn together, and stared at the wall.

"OK," Dr. Lovaas said, and slapped his knees as he stood up. "No go." He turned to me. "You will come back one week from today, agreed?"

"But that's such a long time," I blurted, and felt myself flush.

He laughed. "You are anxious to get started now." He patted my shoulder. "Rest while you can. I have a skiing trip planned--a hold-over from life in Norway. I must have at least one skiing trip a year, or I shrivel up and die." He laughed at his own joke, then became businesslike. "Do not give Drew breakfast or lunch on Wednesday before you bring him in."

"Not feed him?"

"Yes, yes," Dr. Lovaas said. "So he will work for food as a reward." He smiled at me, and patted my arm. "It will be fine. He will not starve."

I could barely prepare myself mentally to allow Drew to work for food, and the idea of him skipping breakfast unsettled me.

"He will be fine," the doctor repeated. "Trust me."

As Drew and I started out the door, Dr. Lovaas spoke again, this time in a hesitant voice. "I do not suppose that you would feel good about allowing Drew to also skip dinner on Tuesday night?" He looked at my face and quickly waved a hand at me. "No, no. I suppose not. Without breakfast will be fine. We will see how well he works for his lunch."

I nodded, but in truth, I didn't look forward to a Drew without breakfast, either.

As we exited Franz Hall, Drew was once again drawn to the fountain. He stood as if mesmerized, until I picked him up and carried him to the car in the parking garage.

When he was settled in his car seat, I dug through my purse for my car keys. As I pulled them out, the sheet of folded paper Andrea had given me was pulled out, too. I hadn't even glanced at it before, but now I unfolded it. As I read the top line, my heart sank. "Early Autism and Childhood Schizophrenia Project."

Gene, with his reluctance to believe anything at all was wrong with Drew, would never sign the form.

Chapter 7

That evening, as I prepared dinner, I glanced at the clock every few minutes. Time crawled until the hands told me it was 5:30. The chain lock was all that stood between Drew and the dangers out doors, so I listened for the sound of the doorbell as I floured liver and sliced onions for Gene's favorite dinner.

When the bell sounded, I ran to answer it. "Hi," I said, and turned my cheek to him for a ritualistic peck.

"Did Drew make any escape attempts today?"

"No, but that doesn't mean he won't," I said, and followed him into the bedroom. On the way, I snatched the folded form off the coffee table and put it behind my back. The idea of a confrontation made my stomach jump, but I mentally prepared myself to do whatever was necessary to see that Gene signed that form.

"Dinner ready?" he asked, as he removed his slacks, shirt and jacket and put on his at-home clothes--faded jeans and a t-shirt.

"About 30 minutes," I said, and swallowed hard.

"What is it?"

I jumped. "What's what?"

He looked at me. "What do you mean, 'Wmacros\hat?' What's dinner? Jesus, Julia."

"Oh, dinner. Liver and onions." I laughed, a jerky little laugh that sounded forced even to my own ears.

He transferred his change, lighter and wallet to the dresser and hung his slacks in the closet. "Liver and onions, huh? So what are you guys eating?"

"Meat loaf," I said, and thrust the form at him. "Here. We need your signature on this before we can start Drew's therapy."

Gene unfolded it, took a pen from the dresser and scribbled his signature on it without so much as a glance at anything but the dotted line. "So they've decided Drew really is autistic, huh?" he asked, and handed me the form as if it was his laundry list.

"Yes," I said, and burst into tears. I didn't know why I cried, whether from nervousness, relief that he had signed the form, or just because I was heartsick and afraid for Drew.

"Don't you cry, Julia," Gene warned, and pointed a finger at me. "Don't you dare cry!"

I slapped at his finger. "I can't help it," I bawled. "I just can't help it."

"Well, pull yourself together. I don't want to hear it," he said, and stalked out of the room.

Angry now, I blew my nose, washed my face and set the table for dinner. We ate in silence, but inside I fumed. How dare he tell me not to cry? Our child had a condition that might result in his being institutionalized for a lifetime, and he was telling me not to cry?

I wanted to dump the mashed potatoes on Gene's head, or bash him in his smug face with a skillet, anything to make him feel what I was feeling. In his own way, my husband was just as unreachable as my son, and both conditions wrenched at my heart.

As we got ready for bed later that evening, Gene sat on the edge of the bed and held one of his socks. He looked up at me as tears slid down his cheeks. "I can't believe there's really something wrong with Drew," he said.

I stared back at him, and all the hurt, the anger, and the heartbreak welled up in me at once. "Don't you dare cry, Gene," I said. "Don't you dare cry."

. . .

The next morning, Gene acted as if nothing had happened, and I tried to act the same way as we packed the car and set off for his parents' home in San Diego.

As we drove down the San Diego Freeway, Drew silently wedged between us, Gene punched the buttons on the radio, moving from station to station and back again. "When does this therapy thing start?" he asked.

I looked up from my book. "Next Wednesday," I said.

"What does he do, go once, twice a week, or what?"

"Six days a week."

He stopped changing stations and looked at me for a moment before he resumed the action. "Six days a week? Are you out of your mind? Who do you think is going to take care of the other kids while you're off gallivanting around?"

"I'm not going to be 'off gallivanting,' as you call it. And anyway, I'll only be gone three days a week--Monday, Wednesday and Friday, while Marie's at school. Tuesday, Thursday and Saturday, the therapy team will come to the house."

He cast an irritated glance at me. "We've got three kids, you know. What about John?"

I pulled a cigarette from my pack and tapped it on my thumbnail. "I told you. Mom and Dad are going to pay to put John in preschool."

"You didn't tell me that. I'm positive. I would've remembered."

"I did. I've told you all this at least once. You just haven't been listening." He mumbled something under his breath. "What? What did you say?"

A muscle jumped in his jaw. "Nothing," he said, and we made the rest of the drive in silence except for the murmurs of Marie and John in the back seat.

. . .

On the day of our first therapy session, I tried to hand Gene the lunch I had packed for him as he was on his way out the door. He stopped and looked at the brown bag, then at me. "What's that?"

"Your lunch. Remember? Dr. Lovaas wants us to be at his office at noon. They're going to see if Drew will work for food. They're all going to bring their lunch, too."

He shook his head. "No. I'm not carrying that."

I pushed it at him again. "Take it, Gene. You have to eat something. You've known about this all along."

"I don't care. I'm not about to carry a brown bag to the office. Nobody else does," he finished in a plaintive voice.

"Oh, for God's sake, how old are you?" I tried to stick the brown bag under his arm.

He let it fall to the floor, and moved toward the door. "No."

I picked it up. "Come on. Put it in your briefcase. No one will know the difference. Anyway, you have to eat. You won't have time to come to Dr. Lovaas's office and go out to get something to eat, too."

He stopped at the door and looked at me. "That's right. I do have to eat. And I don't have time to do both. So I'm not going to be there."

Chapter 8

I couldn't believe my ears. "You promised. You said--"

He shook his head. "I don't care. I can't do without lunch. I'd never make it. And I'm not carrying a brown bag." He set his mouth in a stubborn line. He looked so much like John I would have laughed if I hadn't been so dismayed.

"Oh, for Pete's sake, Gene. If a man with a Ph.d doesn't mind carrying his lunch to the office, why should you?" My voice was almost a shriek by now.

"I'm not doing it," he said, and was out the door before I could argue further.

"Wait. Please. You've got to--" I stopped as he jerked open the car door and threw his briefcase in, then entered the car himself.

I stood in the hallway for a moment holding the useless brown bag in my hand. "How can a grown man be such a big baby," I asked aloud. I shook my head and went to the kitchen to fix breakfast for the kids. I shoved the bag into the refrigerator so hard that the sandwich must have been flattened against the milk, but I didn't care. As I heated the cast iron skillet for the pancake batter I'd prepared earlier, I heard a noise behind me. I turned and saw Drew sitting expectantly in his chair at the table. He watched my every move in obvious anticipation of the breakfast to come.

"Ehhhhh," he said.

I closed my eyes and massaged the bridge of my nose. "Oh, God," I said. "I forgot about Drew not eating." I looked at the bowl of pancake batter, then back to him. Of all the things to fix on a morning when Drew wasn't supposed to eat, pancakes were the worst. He adored pancakes. The closest I ever saw him to delight was when he ate them.

Marie bounded into the kitchen with John on her heels. "Ooh, pancakes!" she squealed. She grabbed Drew in a bear hug. "Pancakes, Drew!"

"Ehhh-hh," came the muffled reply.

With a sigh, I poured the batter into the hot skillet and resigned myself to the battle to come.

He rocked from side to side in his chair and whined, his eyes on the pancake griddle.

"Eh-h-h?"

"No, Honey. You can't eat now. You have to wait till lunch." I slid a pancake onto John's plate.

Drew's dark eyes clouded and his brows drew together. "Eh-h-h-h! Uh-uh-uh-uh." He reached across the table to John's plate.

"No! Mommy, make him quit."

I swatted Drew's hand lightly. "Stop it, now. I'm sorry, but you'll just have to wait." I removed him from the table, but he grabbed his chair and hung on for all he was worth. I tried to pry his fingers loose and he kicked his legs, catching me on the shinbone. "Ow, darn it, Drew." I let go, and he scrambled back up into his chair.

I hesitated a moment, then pulled chair and all away from the table, and moved it closer to the stove. He slid out of it and attempted to pull it out of my grasp. I held on and continued to cook the pancakes one-handed. Drew's shrieks seemed to increase in proportion to the stack of pancakes and my head pounded with the sound of them.

When John and Marie finished eating, I loaded all three children into the car and took Marie to school. When we came back to the house, I settled onto the couch with one of the books I had picked up at the library the day before. I still had two-and-a-half hours to go before we had to be at Dr. Lovaas's office, and I wanted to be prepared when we got there.

I had already read one book about autism by someone with an unpronounceable German name, and now I was well into one by a man named Kanner. It was a little dry and didn't seem to get any less so as I read, but I lit a cigarette and found my place in it. I had to know what I was fighting. After a few more pages, I came to a passage that provoked horror in me. How could this be? This Kanner character, whoever he was, said that autism was caused by the parent. He cited studies showing that autistic children came from cold and callous parents who rarely showed affection to their offspring.

My heart thumped painfully, and a knot formed in my stomach. Dr. Simmons had mentioned the "refrigerator mother" theory, but had not seemed to place much credence in it. What if he was wrong? I was no psychologist, but what Kanner said made sense to me. A cold and unfeeling mother was bound to make an impact on her child, and perhaps that impact would result in a child who could not relate to anyone, who had no feelings for anyone or anything. Like Drew.

"Oh, my God," I said softly. "Could it be me?" I looked at the boys where they sat on the floor before me. Drew spun the wheel on a little car, and John colored intently in a Disney coloring book.

I remembered how I had not at first wanted children, until Gene convinced me to see it his way. I didn't dislike children. I just didn't feel that they had a place in the life plans I had mapped out for myself.

Then, I remembered the first time Marie was placed in my arms. An all-encompassing love had welled up in me at the sight of her. Any other plans I had made for myself left me, and all I wanted was to care for and cherish that tiny, sweet-smelling bundle that lay in my arms. From that moment on, I was a mother first, and everything else came after. I would walk through fire for my children, give my life for them. How could I be responsible for this impenetrable barrier surrounding Drew? A physical pain seemed to radiate from my chest, and I pressed both hands into it to stop it.

John looked up at me from the floor where he lay coloring. "Huh, Mommy?"

"Nothing, Honey," I said in a halting voice. "Mommy's just a little sad." My voice fell to a whisper as tears slid down my cheeks. I looked at Drew where he sat at my feet, still spinning the wheel on the toy car. How could I live with myself if I had done this to him? How could I face the people at Dr. Lovaas's office? The librarian had said this volume was an authoritative book on the subject of autism. Surely every person connected with the Young Autism Project had read it, or at least knew of this guys theory.

John came to the couch and climbed up beside me. He put both arms around me and patted me on the back with his head on my chest. "Poor Mommy," he said, and looked up at me, his face serious. "Remember, I love you, and Drew does, too." He looked at his brother. "Right, Drew?"

"Eight. Nine. Ten," Drew said, and spun the wheel on the car.

John looked back at me. "He does, Mommy." He pointed to his own chest. "Inside, he does."

I hugged John. "I know he does. And I know you do, too." I sent him back to his coloring, and looked from my book to Drew and back again. I knew that no matter what people thought, I would show up at UCLA today and every day I was supposed to, even if I had to crawl. As long as I breathed, I would work to see that Drew recovered, that he had every chance to live normally. No matter what the cost.

By 11:00, I managed to pull myself together and loaded both boys up to take John to Four Square Gospel Church Day Care. As I led him into the detached building behind the church, with Drew on my hip, John clenched my hand tightly. Guilt assailed me as I looked down at him. Would this child suffer the consequences of Drew's illness? I didn't know, and probably wouldn't, until it was too late, but I could think of no alternative. At least the place was cheerful and clean.

I filled out the necessary papers while Drew whined and rocked on my lap. John huddled close to me, and a half dozen children ventured half-way into the room to stare at us. The attendant who greeted us wore a name tag that said, "Miss Donna," and looked quite relieved to find that Drew would not be spending time at the day care center. I had become so used to his nasal whine that I tuned it out on a regular basis, but it seemed that others could not do so.

When I hugged John good-bye, his chin quivered, and I almost backed out, but I knew I had to stick to the decision I had made, whatever the consequences. I kissed him on the forehead and squeezed his sturdy body once more, then hefted Drew onto my hip and made my exit. As I went out into the sunshine, I prayed that the results of Dr. Lovaas's program would be worth the sacrifices we all would make.

I stopped at a fast-food place in Reseda and got Drew a large order of his second favorite food, french fries. If he would work for anything, it would be the crispy potatoes.

I entered the large room with our lunches in hand, and pulled a reluctant Drew behind me. Dr. Lovaas sat among a tangle of video equipment on a white leather couch. The couch made such an incongruous statement in this toy-strewn room that I couldn't believe I hadn't noticed it before.

The doctor's whole left leg was encased in a white plaster cast, but he gave me a huge smile. "Hello, hello," he said. "And how are you, Mrs. Crowder?"

"Julia, please," I said.

"Ah. Julia it is, then."

Several young people sat around the long folding table, and I recognized a few from previous visits, but felt too shy to speak to them. Instead, I eyed the cast on Dr. Lovaas's leg. "What happened to your leg?"

He made a wry face. "My skiing trip was not so successful." He motioned at his leg. "One would never know I have been on the slopes my entire life." He leaned toward Drew. "Hello, young man. How are you today?"

I held to Drew's hand as he turned his head away. Dr. Lovaas smiled and got to his feet. "Today, he will not speak. Someday ... maybe so," he said. "So. We will begin with the Peabody, which Doug will administer."

"What's a Peabody?" I asked as I went to the table and put my lunch and Drew's french fries down.

"It is a vocabulary test, very simple. Doug will say a word, and, theoretically, Drew will tell us what it is. We must know, or attempt to know, at what level Drew now functions." He stood, and took a pair of crutches from under the table. Hobbling in front of me, he said, "Doug will take Drew now, and we will watch."

Doug held his hand out to Drew, who ignored it. Finally, the young man picked him up and I saw Drew's whole body tense. His eyes blackened and he began a steady drone. Doug carried him through another door, adjacent to the one where Dr. Lovaas now stood and waited for me.

I went into the room, followed by dark-haired Andrea, the graduate student I had met on my previous visit, and Dr. Lovaas. The room contained several chairs and a sort of table built along one wall. The wall above the table was taken up by a smoked glass window through which I could see Drew and Doug.

We seated ourselves in front of the counter and looked through the glass. Drew sat at a little table on a child's size chair and struggled to rise. Doug squatted beside him and held him in the chair. A spiral, hard back book lay on the table, and Doug slid it across to where he and Drew were and opened it. "See the pictures, Drew? I'm going to say a word, and you point to the right picture."

Drew slipped under Doug's arm, under the table and out the other side. He ran over to the toys and grabbed a Jack- in-the-box. The strains of "Pop Goes The Weasel" sounded until Doug crossed the room and picked him up. He pried the toy from the child's hand, took him back to the chair and sat him down, then took Drew's hand in his and pointed to the picture of a ball. "Ball, Drew. See? Ball."

Drew's only response was to turn his face as far to the left as he could, away from Doug and the book. Doug moved the book directly in front of Drew, and Drew swiveled his blond head all the way to the right to avoid the pictures again. Doug followed the movement of his head with the book, and took Drew's hand. He moved the hand to the picture of the ball, and at the same time said, "Ball," then, "Go-o-od. That's what I want you to do, touch the ball."

Drew looked at him from the corner of his eyes and gave him a sly, lopsided smile.

Doug flipped the page. "Truck. Touch the truck. Good." Suddenly, Drew ducked under the book and the table, and emerged on the other side.

Beside me, Andrea laughed. "There he goes again. He's a slippery one."

Drew headed for the Jack-in-the-box, but this time, Doug beat him to it. He carried the toy back to the table, and Drew followed him. Doug looked up, toward where we sat behind the window. "Dr. Lovaas, do you want me to go on?"

The doctor leaned forward and pressed the "speak" button on a microphone which sat on the table. "Yes. Try it again."

Doug put the Jack-in-the-box on the table and sat in the little chair himself this time. He attempted to place Drew on his lap, but Drew stiffened his body until he was rigid and at a 45-degree angle from Doug. He tried to get away, but Doug held tight until Drew tired of the struggle and relaxed his body to a sitting position.

Doug held the book in front of Drew's face and said, "Truck." He moved Drew's hand to touch the picture of the truck, and said, "Truck. Goo-od." He flipped the page and moved the little hand to another picture. "Doll. Doll. Good, Drew."

Drew stiffened his body once again. Doug held on, but looked toward the window. "Dr. Lovaas?"

The doctor leaned forward and spoke into the microphone. "That will be enough, Doug. He is not going to cooperate, or he does not know. He may play with the toys for a few minutes now if he wishes."

Dr. Lovaas looked at my face, and must have seen the disappointment written there. He patted my shoulder. "It is all right, Julia. We did not really expect the child to do much more than he did. That is one of the things that makes him autistic. He either cannot or will not follow verbal instructions."

I fidgeted in my chair and wished we'd leave the small room so I could have a cigarette. "I just don't want him to be a zero on a test," I fretted. "He's a little slow, but he's not that bad."

Dr. Lovaas patted my hand then held onto the table and pulled himself to his feet. "We will not make him a zero. We will just write 'untestable' on the profile and not give him a score at all."

I preceded him through the door and lit a cigarette. I saw Doug emerge from the room where he and Drew had been. He now carried the little table, which he sat down near the toy box at the opposite end of the room from where I stood.

Dr. Lovaas, Andrea, and one of the other graduate students stood in a small knot, and spoke softly to one another. I walked over to the door Doug had emerged from and looked in at Drew. He sat in the middle of the floor playing with the Jack-in-the-box, his blond hair sticking up in spikes, mussed from his struggles with Doug.

Doug brushed by me with a folding chair, which he set up a few feet in front of a couch, the room's only other furniture. He stopped a moment, looked around him, and muttered, "I guess that's about it." He looked up at me and blushed. "Talking to myself," he said.

I cupped my hand and flipped my ashes into it, and tried to smile. "What now?" I asked.

"We're going to check out Drew's reaction to strangers."

"Oh." It sounded like a weird test to me, but then, so did everything else here. Doug brushed by me again, and I glanced at Drew, who was trying to stuff a block into the small space where the clown went in the Jack-in-the-box. I wandered back into the large room, feeling jittery and restive.

Every time I looked at Andrea or Doug or one of the other student-volunteers, I wondered if they knew it was my fault Drew was autistic. And if they did, what must they think of me? I felt miserable and alone. If I had caused Drew's problems, would the therapy really do any good? Maybe I needed therapy so I wouldn't do him any more harm.

My thoughts were interrupted by Dr. Lovaas. "Julia, Here is what I want you to do. Go into the room where Drew is, and sit in the folding chair Doug has placed there. Ignore Drew, until I tell you otherwise. I will instruct you, via the microphone."

I nodded, went to the table and put my cigarette out, then went back into the room. At the doorway, I stopped and looked back. "Should I close it?"

Dr. Lovaas nodded as he made his way to the adjoining room. I closed the door and sat down in the folding chair. Drew cranked the Jack-in-the-box, and the tinny treble of "Pop Goes the Weasel" grated on my raw nerves.

"All right, Julia," came Dr. Lovaas's disembodied voice. "Call him to you."

I cleared my throat a little self-consciously. "Uh, Drew. Come here, Honey." He ignored me. "Drew. Come to Mommy." He continued to play on, and I looked toward the glass window.

"See if you can get him to play with you," said Dr. Lovaas.

I sat still for a moment. What did all this have to do with autism? I wondered. I sighed and shook my head. I guess they know what they're doing, I thought. I went to the corner and got a multicolored ball, about the size of a basketball. Squatting, I rolled it toward Drew. "Want to play ball with Mommy?" I asked. He ignored me as the ball bumped him and rebounded to me. I rolled it again, a little harder this time. Still no reaction.

"All right, Julia. That will be fine. Now, I want you to leave the room. You may come in here if you like, so you can see what is happening."

My knees popped as I stood, and I winced. I glanced at Drew, then left him there and closed the door softly behind me. In the other room, I watched through the glass as someone I had never seen entered and sat down. She looked to be in her mid-twenties, and I figured her for another graduate student.

She sat still for a few minutes, then called Drew to her. He ignored her as he had me, and she tried again. Still he ignored her. Dr. Lovaas spoke into the microphone. "See if you can get him to play, Tina."

The young woman attempted to get his attention with various toys, but Drew acted as if he didn't even see her.

Dr. Lovaas looked at me. "Go back in now, but do not say anything. Just sit on the couch while Tina attempts to interact with Drew."

After I entered the room, Tina tried various ploys to engage Drew in a one-to-one activity, to no avail. She looked up at the window.

"Very well, Tina," Dr. Lovaas said. "You may go. Thank you." There was a pause while Tina made her exit, then I heard Dr. Lovaas's voice again. "Julia, try to make Drew angry."

I frowned. "Make him angry?"

"Yes. Take the toy from him or something. Make him angry."

Still doubtful, I went across the room, and took the Jack-in-the-box from him. Drew looked at the space in front of him for some time as if the toy were still there, then looked up and slightly to my right.

"Eh-h-h."

I shook my head. "No toy."

"EH-H-H," he said, louder this time. When I still withheld the toy from him, he fell to the floor and gave a few half-hearted kicks, then lay still, a low whine coming from his throat.

"Does he normally tantrum when he does not get his way?" Dr. Lovaas asked.

I shook my head. "Not usually. This is about as far as he ever goes." I remembered the battle we fought earlier, and added, "Unless it's about food."

"Can you get him to laugh?"

I looked at Drew where he still lay on the floor, his black eyes smoldering as he looked at the ceiling. "I doubt it."

Dr. Lovaas paused, then said, "Well, try anyway."

I felt like a fool as I tickled Drew, and, when that failed, made faces at him. As usual, he went all out to avoid my face.

"All right, Julia. That's enough," said Dr. Lovaas.

I nodded, but didn't leave the room. My God, I thought as I picked up Drew, his body stiff and unyielding. What have I gotten myself into? How is this going to help Drew? Maybe I'm the one with the problem. First I give him autism, and if that's not bad enough, I take him to a group of people with some very weird ideas of what therapy entails. As the questions and accusations spun in my head, I heard Andrea's voice at the door and turned to look at her.

"I'm ready for Drew now," she said, and motioned to the larger room. "We do therapy out here." She turned to go, then looked back to me. "Did you bring something for him to eat?"

I nodded and picked Drew up. He stiffened his body and made it hard for me to hold him. "There are french fries in that sack on the table," I said.

She nodded as I followed her out of the room. "Ok." She motioned to a small chair. "You can just set him there." She went to the table and brought back the french fries, and sat down in another small chair opposite the one I was trying to keep Drew in.

I looked around, and saw that almost everyone was clustered around the long table a short distance away. The only exception was a young man amid the maze of wires and video equipment. He looked through a view-finder and seemed to find what he saw agreeable. He turned a switch, and I heard a faint whirring noise.

Drew had spied the french fries in Andrea's hand, and now seemed willing to stay in the chair. I stood behind him, unsure of what I should be doing. Dr. Lovaas motioned to me and patted a chair beside him. "Come sit by me, Julia."

I glanced at Drew one last time. His eyes were riveted on Andrea's hands as she broke several of the french fries into tiny pieces. I went to the chair the doctor had indicated and sank into it.

"This is all very strange to you, is it not?" he asked, and the compassion in his eyes almost reduced me to tears.

I managed a smile back, but inside, doubts continued to plague me. I felt up, energized, and this Young Autism Project really intrigued me, but how could I know this was the right program for Drew? I sighed and turned toward Andrea and Drew.

They sat in the tiny chairs, knees touching. Drew's gaze was still glued to the french fries Andrea held in her left hand. With her right, she touched her nose with her fingers. "Touch nose," she said.

Drew remained motionless, eyes on the french fries. Andrea took one tiny piece of potato and held it to the side of her left eye. "Look!" she said. Drew raised his eyes to the french fry and Andrea smiled and popped it into his mouth, and at the same time, patted his leg and said, "Goo-o-d," just as I had noticed Dr. Lovaas saying on an earlier visit.

I frowned as I watched Andrea touch her nose again and repeat her earlier command. "Touch nose," she said.

I looked at Dr. Lovaas, and he grinned. "I suppose you would like to know what she is doing with your child."

"I wouldn't mind."

He looked back to Andrea and Drew, then at Doug. "She will need you. Drew will not model the behavior, I do not think."

Doug nodded, and went to Drew. He crouched behind Drew's chair, and grasped Drew's right hand. This time, when Andrea touched her nose and gave the command, Doug brought my son's little hand up to touch his nose. As Drew touched his nose, Andrea popped a piece of french fry into his mouth, patted him on the leg, and said, "Go-o-od," at almost exactly the same time.

Dr. Lovaas leaned toward me and motioned to the scene in front of us. "We must show the child exactly what we want from him. If he does not respond to modeling, as Andrea was doing, we prompt him, as Doug is now doing. Then, when Drew touches his nose, we reward him with the food. We must do so within two seconds of his response."

"This is behavior modification?" I asked. "Like I read in the book you gave me?"

He nodded. "Yes."

"But they train dogs like this," I protested.

He nodded. "And people, too. It is sound, and is backed by much empirical data. We reward good behavior immediately with a reinforcer and an approving response, and soon, we will dispense with the food as reinforcer."

Still doubtful, I looked at Andrea, Doug, and Drew. "Why do you all speak to him like that?" The loudness of Andrea's voice, both in commands and approval, seemed to me that it would scare Drew, although he seemed unruffled.

"Everything must be larger than life for the autistic child," Dr. Lovaas said. "It is as if they are deep in a tunnel where sight and sound barely penetrate. We must exaggerate our voice and our motions to reach them."

I heard crying and looked at Drew. He rocked his body sideways to try to escape Doug's grasp, and Andrea continued to try to get his attention. "Look!" she commanded, with a french fry held close to her eye, but Drew twisted violently and fell from Doug's grasp onto the floor. Doug started to pick him up, but Dr. Lovaas stopped him.

"I think he is too tired, now. Obtain a positive response, and we will stop for today."

Andrea returned to the previous command of "Touch nose!" and Doug prompted the correct response. Both chorused, "Go-ood," and Andrea gave Drew a tiny piece of potato.

Dr. Lovaas turned to me. "This has been very hard on both of you. Why don't you take Drew home and both of you rest? We will begin again tomorrow."

"All right," I said, but I wondered if I could force myself to go through this again the next day. I hadn't realized it would be such an ordeal. I started toward where Drew sat sniffling on the floor, eating the remaining french fries, then stopped and turned around. Dr. Lovaas bent over a notebook, intent on whatever entry he was making.

"Doctor?" I bit my lip and shifted from foot to foot.

He turned to look at me. "Yes?"

I looked at Drew's tear-streaked face, then back to Dr. Lovaas. Could I stand to know if I had caused Drew's autism? I stood silent for a moment, embarrassed before the doctor and these young people who looked at me so expectantly. Finally, I sighed. "Nothing," I said. "Never mind." Right now, I didn't want to know, and the heavy mantle of cowardice made my shoulders sag, even more than the guilt.

At home that night, with Marie, John, and the exhausted Drew long asleep, Gene surprised me by asking how Drew's first day of therapy went.

I thought for a moment, then said, "It was--tiring, I guess." I explained what had taken place, and he listened intently, nodding here and there.

When I finished, he said, "Well, it sounds like you've got it all under control."

I lit a cigarette and leaned against the back of the couch as I inhaled. "I don't know about that. Right now it seems like an overwhelming proposition."

Gene surprised me by scooting closer and putting his arm around me. "I'll help," he said. "You won't be in it by yourself."

Grateful for the support, I leaned into him and tried to believe that instead of being torn apart, our family might be drawn closer together by the demands of Drew's treatment. I put any doubt out of my mind, storing it in the same dusty room with my fears about my culpability for Drew's condition.

Part II

Treatment

Chapter 9

EXCERPT FROM PARENT THERAPY LOG

February 20, 1975

Drew put his coat on right-side up today. He had a small tantrum this afternoon, and hit himself in the head. He's never done that before. Is it significant?

February 21, 1975

Today was the first session at home. It was tiring, a little stressful for both of us.

February 22, 1975

The session at UCLA today ran from noon till 2 p.m. He cried a lot the first hour and fell asleep once. He called me "Mama" once when he was crying and twice more this evening. I guess I should be thrilled, since it's the first time, but it's a drop in the bucket as far as what remains to be learned.

The days seemed to run together after we became adjusted to the routine of therapy, but a few stood out from the others. The day Andrea, whom I now called Andi, Laurie and Martha came to the house for the first time was more than a little nerve-wracking for me. I had long since committed myself to Dr. Lovaas's program, but as I waited for them to appear at my door, I began to wonder if Gene was right when he objected to the presence of the therapy team in our home.

At the thought of Gene, resentment bubbled up inside me. He should be here, I thought, with a kind of loneliness mingled with the resentment. I suppressed them both and put on a smile as I opened the door to admit Andi and the others.

When we discussed the visits to the house, Andi had stressed over and over that I was not to go to any additional trouble cleaning up in preparation. "Honest, Julia," she had said, "Don't go running around picking up before we come. Just let everything be as natural as possible."

Easy for her to say, I thought now as I ushered the three of them into the living room. She'd probably never seen the damage three kids could do to a house. Things I didn't ordinarily notice, like the coffee table with its scratches, the curtain-less back door, and the breakfast dishes in the sink, all seemed to shout out the presence of a careless housekeeper.

When we were in the living room, I excused myself, and said, "I'll get Drew." I padded down the hallway to the boys' bedroom. Company always sent Drew into hiding, and today was no exception.

John sat on the floor of the bedroom with a pile of Lincoln Logs from which he was constructing a long, low building. He looked up as I entered. "You want to help me, Mommy?"

I squatted beside him. "What are you making?"

He fit together another pair of brown, notched logs. "A house for martians." *My Favorite Martian* was far and away his favorite show. I often came upon him standing in front of an object with his finger pointed toward it and a familiar beeping noise coming from him as he pretended to move the object by levitation.

"Do you want to help me?" he asked again.

"I can't, Honey. Not right now, anyway. Drew's therapy team is here."

He knit his brows together. "What's a ferapy team?"

I smiled and ruffled his short blond hair. "Remember? It's Andi, from Dr. Lovaas's office. And Laurie and Martha. They're going to help make Drew all better." I straightened up and ruffled his hair again. "Then you'll have somebody to play with."

"Yeah. Somebody to play with," he repeated, and fit another two logs together.

I went toward the closet. "Drew's in there," John said from behind me. "He don't want you to get him."

"Mm-hm," I said, as I slid open the closet door and plucked one of my old sweaters off the pile on the floor. Drew looked up at me from where he lay, his eyes enormous and dark. They never met mine, and I always had the disconcerting feeling that he was looking at someone just over my shoulder. I held out my hand. "Come on, big guy. Time to go to work."

He turned his face toward the wall, and I could see his body arch and tense. Sighing, I squatted and picked up his unyielding form.

In the living room, I deposited him on the couch. "He may not be very cooperative," I said.

"We'll do fine," Andi assured me. "He hasn't eaten yet, has he?"

I rolled my eyes. "No, but what a battle it was. I thought if I got John and Marie up a little early and fed them before he got up I could get away with it." I went to the end of the couch. "No chance. I think he's got a built-in alarm of some kind--lets him know when it's time to eat or watch *Bowling For Dollars*." I knelt down and peered into the dim recess.

"He watches TV?" Laurie's surprised voice came from the couch.

"M-hm," I said, "but just *Bowling For Dollars*."

"So what does he do?" Laurie asked. "Just come in and turn it on, or what?" She tilted her head to one side, and the overhead light glinted off her shiny blonde hair.

I tapped a cigarette on my thumbnail. "Every night at 7:00 he just goes to the TV and stands in front of it until someone turns it on. Then he stands and watches it till it's over." I lit the cigarette and grinned through the smoke at Laurie. I felt strangely proud of Drew's little eccentricity. He might be autistic, but he wasn't without character.

Laurie and Martha looked at each other, then at me. "Far out," Martha said.

Laurie looked around the living room. "Isn't John home?"

I nodded. "He's in his room, playing."

"Why don't you bring him in?" Andi said, looking up from where she sat on the floor with Drew. "This is a family affair, after all."

"You're sure it's OK? I thought of taking him to a baby sitter, but it's Saturday, and he's gone so much now ..." My voice trailed off, but guilt made my stomach cramp. I had been so wrapped up in Drew's treatment that I didn't get to spend as much time as I thought I should with John and Marie, and it gnawed at me.

"Of course it's OK. It's great, as a matter of fact." Andi flipped her hair over her shoulder, making sure to keep one hand around Drew's arm. "We just want everything to be as normal as possible. Home therapy is one of the things that makes Dr. Lovaas's program unique, and what's a home without a family? Bring John in, and Marie, too, if she's here."

I shook my head. "She's down the street at a friend's, but I'll get John." I went down the hall and returned with John, who clutched a Lincoln Log in one fist and looked at our guests with big eyes.

"Hi, John," Andi said. "Do you remember me?"

John looked up at me, then at Andi, and nodded. When I sat on the floor cross-legged, he did the same.

Andi stayed on the floor with Drew in front and facing her. She held up a tiny piece of cookie near her right eye. "Touch nose," she said.

Drew ignored the command, but Martha sat behind him, caught his hand in hers and brought it up to do as Andi said. When he had touched his nose, Andi popped the cookie into his mouth. "Go-ood," she said.

"Um," Drew replied, and smacked his lips over the tidbit. A dozen or more times, Martha prompted Drew to touch his nose. Each time, Andi popped a little piece of cookie into his mouth and said, "Goo-ood." Drew seemed to be more a little more cooperative now.

After many trials, Drew touched his nose on command unaided. I saw both Andi's and Martha's faces light up. "Goo-ood, Drew," they cried in unison. "That's good."

In spite of my resolve not to get my hopes up, the light in their faces ignited hope within me. I sat tensely on the floor and urged Drew on.

As if responding to my encouragement, he touched his nose by himself a few times, then began to ignore the command.

"Touch nose!" Andi said again, but Drew still ignored her. "No!" Andi said, and her voice took on a sharp sound I hadn't heard before. She took his hand and roughly moved it up to his nose. "I hope he's not satiated," she said, and looked at Martha. "That happens sometimes. They just get full if it's food, or bored with it if it's something else." She gave Drew the command again, and again he ignored her. "No!" she said, even more sharply, and moved his hand to his nose.

I winced with each "No!" and wanted to stop the action immediately, but I steeled myself. It might be unpleasant, but if that's what it took to make him well, I could stand it.

"We've got to get him to do it just once more on his own so we can quit. Never stop on a negative note," she said, and both Laurie and Martha nodded. "Touch nose," Andi said, and, finally, Drew touched his nose unaided.

"All right!" Laurie said, and clapped her hands.

We all chorused, "Go-ood, Drew, that's goo-od!"

Andi stood, followed shortly by Martha and Laurie. "A super session," she said. "Really super."

I looked at my watch and was surprised to see that over two hours had passed. "Gosh," I said. "I didn't realize how late it was."

Andi nodded. "You really get wrapped up in the intensity of the situation."

"You sure do," I said. I was beginning to understand the behavior modification techniques, but after each session, I felt like I had been in a fight. My shoulders ached from tension, and sometimes I had deep indentations in my palms from clenching my hands. Still, with each session, I became more and more convinced that this treatment was going to work.

As I saw the women to the door, Andi bent over and ruffled John's hair. "You're a pretty handsome guy, you know that, Munchkin?"

John grinned and ducked his head. "No, I'm not. I'm Mr. Spock." He grasped the tops of his ears and pulled them to a point. "See my ears?"

All three young women laughed, and Andi said, "Beam me up, Scotty."

John's mouth rounded in an "O," and he looked up at me. "She knows Star Trek," he said, and looked back at her in evident awe.

We all laughed, and in a burst of hyperactivity, John darted across the living room and pointed a Lincoln Log at various objects while emitting staccato bursts of sound. Drew watched in silence from just inside the kitchen, his face devoid of expression.

As I was about to shut the door behind Andi and the others, she called to Laurie and Martha, "You two go ahead, I'll be right there." She returned to where I stood at the door. "Julia, I was just wondering how your husband feels about Drew's treatment."

My heart sank as I attempted to form an answer to her question. Could they refuse to treat Drew if Gene refused to participate?

Chapter 10

I avoided Andi's curious dark eyes and studied the porch. "He's--he had to go to San Diego for the weekend." I felt the heat rise in my face and willed her to believe me. I couldn't stand it if Gene's refusal to take part caused Drew to be dropped from the program. Anger at him welled up in me, but I tried to remain calm as I looked into Andi's eyes. "Maybe he can be here next time," I said. I knew he probably wouldn't be, but I resolved then and there that nothing could induce me to stop now. Drew's treatment would continue, come Hell or high water. If Gene wouldn't participate, I'd do his share too, and deal with the issue of why he didn't help later.

Andi patted my shoulder as if she had read my mind. "This is rough on a family. But don't worry. You'll make it. It's no big deal, and really none of my business, ok?"

After they had gone, I leaned against the door. Somehow, I would keep Drew in the Young Autism program. At that moment, I didn't care what sacrifice I had to make. I would make it, with or without Gene.

. . .

At Monday's session, Gene was far from my thoughts. The question of the origin of Drew's disability still gnawed at me. Knowing could not be worse than wondering.

"Is this my fault?" I asked.

"This?" Dr. Lovaas pulled his gaze from where Laurie sat knee to knee with Drew. Andi squatted and held Drew in place. Drew cried and tried to twist himself away from her, but she held tight.

"No!" Laurie said when Drew refused to obey the command. She looked at Andi for approval, then raised Drew's hand roughly to his nose.

Andi nodded. "Ok. Super. Just keep your voice firm, and force his hand up. You're not hurting him, I promise."

I deliberately turned from the scene. I hated it when Drew cried. I knew he didn't understand why people wouldn't leave him alone, and it broke my heart to see him so confused and unhappy.

"Julia?" Dr. Lovaas looked at me in puzzlement. "You were speaking?"

"Do they have to keep at him?" I asked, momentarily forgetting my question. My heart felt like it was being wrenched from my chest, and I jumped a little each time the tone of his cries changed.

"Yes, they do. It would be more cruel to stop," Dr. Lovaas replied. "He likes his safe little world, and he does not want us in it. So, he cries."

"I still don't like it."

"You do not have to like it, but you will become accustomed to it." He patted my knee. "What were you going to say? Before."

"Oh. I checked some books out of the library, about autism, and one of them said that parents cause it. It said the mothers are cold and un--""

He looked at me with just a touch of irritation. "Who was it? Kanner?" he asked.

I looked at him blankly, and he repeated it.

"Kanner. Was it his book that you read?"

"I'm not sure. That might have been it. I've read a couple. He said that cold and unloving parents cause autism in their children."

"I do not believe that," Dr. Lovaas said. "'Refrigerator mothers' is what he calls them. Believe me, Julia. You have not caused your son's condition. We do not know what causes it, but you did not. That we know." He peered at me. "How long have you worried about this?"

"Only since last week."

He smiled at me, and squeezed my hand. "That is too long. You must not try to take the blame for this."

"If you're sure."

"I am sure. I will not lie to you."

"All right," I said, but the words failed to convey what I felt just then. It was as if a damp, smelly weight had been lifted from me. Maybe I wasn't the world's best mother, but at least I hadn't done anything to cause my son to withdraw into a shell of autism.

I savored the relief for a few moments while I watched the therapy team work with Drew. Without that guilt weighing me down, I even felt that I could stand the crying.

Dr. Lovaas heaved himself from his chair and hobbled across the room to where Andi now stood, looking down at Laurie and Drew. Dr. Lovaas turned and motioned to me. "Come, Julia. It is your turn."

My heart lurched, and my stomach felt as if it dropped to my feet. "My turn? You're kidding. I'm no therapist."

"Ah, but you are," Dr. Lovaas said. "All my parents are therapists. My best mothers just jump right in, right from the beginning."

I lit a cigarette with shaking hands. I wanted to be one of his best mothers, maybe even the best mother. I just didn't want to do it with everybody looking at me. "I don't think I can."

Laurie came across the room. "Sure you can. It's easy. We're all learning." She pulled me back to where Andi, Drew and Dr. Lovaas were. Drew whined and twisted almost out of Andi's grasp.

"Mama," he said, quite clearly.

I looked down at him in astonishment, then up at Dr. Lovaas and Andi. Andi seemed to catch it at once. "He's never said 'Mama' before, has he? I can see it in your face!"

I shook my head. "It's a first," I agreed, but I couldn't work up as much enthusiasm as I would've thought. All I could think of was what a very small step it was, and how much remained to be accomplished. "It's a start," I said, and lowered myself to the floor. Over the nervous lump in my throat, I said, "Touch nose!"

Chapter 11

February 24, 1975
No crying.
Still resisted looking on command.
Learned imitation
1) arms out--few prompts
2) tap knees--few prompts
3) touch head--got it on trial 1
4) tap table--got it on trial 1
Could alternate all of these with few mistakes!
Lots of talking and looking during this.
U.C.L.A.
February 26, 1975
Worked on responding to verbal cues.
1) touch your nose
2) touch your eye
3) touch your ear
4) touch your head
5) tap the table
He cried for five minutes near the end. Julia worked with him. She's great on positives, will need some work on negatives.

"Touch nose!" With my face mere inches from Drew's, I made my voice as firm as possible. He turned his face away from me.

"No!" I said. My intended sharpness didn't come through, and, with angry but tearless eyes, Drew tried to twist out of Laurie's grip.

Andi knelt beside me. "Just get him to do something so we can quit. He's getting tired."

"Touch knee," I said, but it took three more trials before Drew would do so. "Go-ood!" I told him, and tried to gather him into my arms, but he struggled from me and crawled a few feet away, where he lay in a sniffling heap.

Andi patted me. "He'll be OK in a few minutes." She offered her hand and I took it. She pulled me to my feet and I went to the table and dug through my purse for a cigarette. I tapped it on my thumbnail and lit it, then blew the smoke out before I spoke.

"This is so hard," I said. "He's just too pitiful when he gets like this."

"Wouldn't it be more pitiful if he were like this at 25?"

I looked at Andi, but her bland face told me nothing. I looked back to Drew. He had recovered and played on the floor with a friction toy. He ran the cars wheels over the tile floor a few times and released it. It raced across the floor to the wall, where it hit and flipped over, wheels spinning. That's the way I feel, I thought. Racing around, feeling like I'm really doing some good, and I'm just spinning my wheels.

The pace of Drew's treatment was grueling. It didn't just take place two hours a day at the clinic or at our home. It was a continual experience. Every opportunity had to be taken by each member of our family to teach Drew some facet of living. In this way, we were teaching him what other children learned just by being.

Yesterday was a typical day. At 7:30 a.m., I was blasted out of a sound sleep by the sounds of the Rolling Stones on my bedside clock radio. I turned it down and lay in the empty bed--Gene was usually long gone when the rest of us awoke--and hummed along with the song. I savored the quiet, and knew these would be my last moments alone until I fell into bed at eleven that night.

Finally, I sat up and stretched, then padded down the hallway to the kitchen. As I poured a cup of coffee from the pot Gene had left plugged in, I glanced at the clock on the wall. 7:45. Perhaps I could squeeze in another few minutes of quiet time. I picked up the list I had made yesterday and, coffee and cigarettes in hand, moved to the rocker in a corner of the kitchen.

I scanned the list. I found out early in Drew's treatment that a list helped me to be more focused and reminded me that I had no time to waste. Today's was lengthy, but no more so than any other day's.

Marie had to be at school by 8:30, and John to preschool by 9:00. Then I needed to pick up some fabric at a local discount store for an outfit I was making for Marie. Drew and I would need to leave Reseda by eleven in order to make it to UCLA in time for therapy. I made a mental note to leave even earlier today--a news report the evening before said that gay rights activists were picketing the psychology building because of another ongoing program. "I hope we don't have trouble crossing the line," I muttered, a little annoyed. I felt little for or against gay rights. I just didn't have the time to waste.

Just then, John came through the kitchen door. "Hi, Mommy. Where's breakfast?"

"Come give me a hug and I'll tell you." I stubbed out my cigarette and held my arms open to him. He moved over to me, yawning and rubbing his eyes, then snuggled up. I kissed the top of his head. Nothing could be sweeter than holding a just-awakened child, I thought.

"Where's breakfast?" John prompted.

I kissed the top of his head again, and patted him on behind. "Breakfast is coming right up," I said. "Go wake Drew up."

"Marie, too?" His black eyes sparkled.

"No. You know she hates it when you--" Before I could finish, he was on his way out of the kitchen.

"Marie-e-e-e, Mommy said get u-u-u-p," he screamed, his voice rising on the last word. He threw a grin over his shoulder at me and I shook my head. It was going to be a long day.

In a few moments, John ran back into the kitchen. "I waked 'em up, Mommy," he informed me as he climbed into his chair.

Drew came in, clutching a small metal car in his hand. I placed a bowl in front him. "Bowl," I said.

"Bowl," Drew said.

"Good talking, Drew," I said, and placed a bowl in front of John. "Bowl," I repeated.

Marie came through the kitchen door, fully dressed. "I hate it," she said as she sat down. "He always screams in my ear and tries to pull off my blanket." She gave John a disgusted look.

"Do not," John said. His grin gave him away.

I set a bowl in front of Marie. "Bowl," I said.

"Bowl," Drew repeated.

"Good talking, Drew," I said.

John clapped his hands. "Good talking, Drew," he enthused, and was seconded by Marie.

I touched Drew's bowl. "What's this?" I asked.

"Bowl," he replied, and grinned at me.

I ruffled his blond head. "Good talking!" I said, and each of the other children echoed my statement.

I placed a spoon at each child's place, and named it each time I laid one down. "Spoon," I said.

"'poon," Drew repeated.

John grabbed Marie's spoon and held it up. "What's this, Drew?"

Marie grabbed for it. "Give it to me, John."

John tried to hold it out of her reach, but Marie went around the table and grabbed it from him.

Marie gave John a withering look. "You act so stupid."

John grinned and picked up the box of Lucky Charms. "Lucky Charms," he said as he dumped some into his bowl. "I lo-o-ve Lucky Charms." He carefully set the box on the side farthest from his sister.

"Charms," Drew said, and waited for cereal.

"Mom, puh-leeze make him give me the cereal. I'm going to be late," Marie implored.

I glanced at the clock. Sure enough, it was five after eight already. I crossed the kitchen and took the cereal box. As I filled Marie's and Drew's bowls, I held up a spoon. "What's this, Drew?"

He looked blank for a moment, then a huge grin spread over his face and he clapped his hands together once. "'poon!" he cried.

"Good talking," I said, and my words were seconded by Marie and John, for once in agreement.

Fifteen minutes later, Marie was off to school, a block and a half away, and I carried Drew into his and John's bedroom. "You come on, too, John," I called over my shoulder.

I sat Drew on the end of the bottom bunk and dug in the chest of drawers for socks, shorts and a shirt. I went back to the bed and held one sock up. "What's this?"

"Sock," he said.

"Good talking," I told him, and went through the same with his shorts and shirt.

John came in and began to dress himself in mismatched shorts and shirt, and I glanced at my watch. "Oh, Lord," I said aloud. "You're going to be late again, John."

"Yeah," he said, and sat down on the bottom bunk next to Drew and me. "I'm always being late. Miss Pam calls me 'Little Boy Late."

I sighed. "Too much to do and not enough time to do it," I muttered.

"Huh?" John looked up and I saw that his shoes were on the wrong feet.

I switched them. "Nothing, Honey." I stood him on his feet and ran to my own room to get dressed.

. . .

Drew and I dropped John off at preschool and drove to TG&Y to select some fabric. In the store, I put Drew in the shopping cart's child-seat and we went to the fabric department. As I wound through the aisles of brightly colored material, Drew watched everything through shining dark eyes.

More and more, I could see the hidden child within my son emerging. I rejoiced in the emergence, and at the same time maintained a superstitious fear that admitting his improvement would somehow end it.

I mused over this knowledge as we came upon a stack of broadcloth. Drew reached out and touched a bolt of red cloth. "Red?" he asked.

My heart leapt. A question! Drew had asked a question, sort of. This was marvelous. "Yes!" I said, and took his face between my hands and kissed his nose. "Yes, yes, yes! Red! Good talking, Drew." The smile on my face seemed to stretch entirely around my head.

A woman in brush rollers sidled past me, a look of distrust on her face. I ignored her and touched another bolt of cloth. "What color?"

"Blue."

"Good talking, Son. Good talking!" Ivar and Andi and the rest of the therapy team will be thrilled, I thought.

Drew touched another bolt of cloth. "This? Red?"

I nearly jumped up and down. He had asked a question! Well, sort of a question--at least it was closer than he had ever come before to asking one.

As I looked at the pink fabric, I realized that this positive leap had come equipped with a built-in pitfall. We had not progressed past the primary colors yet. I hesitated a moment, then said, "Pink." I touched the cloth. "Pink," I repeated.

Confusion crept over his face like a shadow and his gaze flicked from the material to me and back again.

I moved the pink bolt next to the red one. I placed his hand on the pink material and said, "Pink." Then I placed his hand on the red. "Red." I did it again. "Pink. Red."

Drew's gaze moved from one bolt to the other as I spoke. Suddenly, his vision cleared and a grin replaced his look of confusion. "Pink!" he shouted. He touched each bolt of material in turn. "Pink. Red. Pink. Red."

For the next hour, our errand was forgotten as we stood amid the bolts of brightly colored cloth, he asking and me naming the colors. By the time we left the store, he could identify pink, white, black, turquoise and orange. Best of all, it had not been forced down his throat. He had initiated it. I could almost believe that his future was as bright as the colors of the fabrics we left behind.

. . .

When we arrived at Ivar's clinic, I bubbled over with our good news. Andi, Howard and the others congratulated Drew, and Howard swooped him up. He traveled around the room with Drew on his shoulders. "Good talking, Drew! All right!" he said, amid Drew's shrieks of delight at the ride.

We were finally able to settle down to work and the next two hours passed in a blur.

At two, Drew and I left for Reseda. We had forty-five minutes in which to pick up John and get home to welcome Marie after school. We made it through the back gate and in the back door just as Marie banged in the front door.

John traipsed through the kitchen with a neighbor child. "Can we have some cookies in the tent?" he asked.

"Sure, but just one each." I doled them out. "And take Drew with you," I said.

His brows drew together. "I always have to take Drew everywhere."

I shrugged. "That's the rule. Where you go, he goes."

"I don't like that rule," he grumbled. "He doesn't even play."

"Sorry," I replied. "Marie? Do want a cookie?"

She sighed and tossed her blonde hair over her shoulder. "I guess, but I have to talk to you about my costume for the play."

"Fine. What about it?" She had talked of little but the coming Girl Scout skit for the last three weeks.

"Mo-o-om. I need a motorcycle jacket. How can I be Fonzie's little brother without a motorcycle jacket?" she asked.

I led Drew out the door and John took him from there. "Sis, I'm not going to buy you a leather jacket for a Girl Scout skit."

"But--"

"No buts. One, we don't have the money, and two, it isn't necessary." I turned back toward the house and she followed.

"I'll be the goofiest looking person there if I don't have a jacket. I'm sure Fonzie will have one." She banged the door behind her. "Mom? Are you listening to me?"

I sighed and turned to her in exasperation. "Yes, Marie, I'm listening to you. I don't have another thing in the world to do but stand here and listen to you argue with me about a jacket you do not need." I paused. "Where is your imagination? If you can pretend to be a boy, can't you pretend to be wearing a motorcycle jacket?"

She flopped down in a kitchen chair a put her head on her folded arms. "You just don't understand."

I sighed and went to a message board on the wall. "Look. I'll find something I can convert to a motorcycle jacket or something, OK?" I penciled in "jacket--second-hand store--" between "John--dentist," and "therapy team -- here." Still, I didn't know where the time would come from. "Just because I can squeeze it in on the board doesn't mean I can squeeze it in for real," I muttered.

I lit a cigarette and started for the utility room. As I passed the garbage can, I stopped and sniffed the air, then stepped on the lever that raised the lid on the plastic container. The bag was filled to overflowing so I picked it up and reversed my steps to the back door to take it out. I sidestepped John and a neighborhood child as they traipsed into the house, Drew in tow. As I returned, they passed me again, this time with arms full of Tonka Trucks and a few smaller vehicles.

In the kitchen once more, I surveyed the number of dirty dishes that now sat on the cabinet and lit another cigarette. I filled the dishwasher and started it, put another plastic bag in the garbage can, and went to put on a load of clothes to wash.

I glanced at the clock as I re-entered the kitchen and groaned. "4:30 already," I said, and went to the back door. "Drew? Come help Mommy fix dinner." I waited to see if he would come on his own or if I needed to go after him. I watched him emerge from the tent and run toward me. I held the door open and ruffled his white-blonde hair as he came in. I closed the door behind him, picked him up and sat him on the cabinet. "Okey-doke," I said. "Let's make a salad." I brought an armful of lettuce, tomatoes, cucumbers and radishes from the refrigerator. "Lettuce," I said as I tore it into pieces.

"Lettuce," Drew answered.

"Good talking, Drew. Cucumber," I said, and held it up for his inspection before I cut it up into the bowl before me.

"Cucumber."

"Good talking."

When the salad was finished, I put Drew on my hip and went to put the clothes in the dryer. "Washer," I said, and put his hand on it.

"Washer," he repeated.

"Dryer." I placed his hand on the ancient white machine.

"Dryer."

I put his hand on the washer. "What's this?"

"Washer," he said.

"Good talking, Drew!"

We went back to the kitchen and put potatoes on to fry, a pre-cooked ham in the oven, and canned vegetables in a saucepan atop the stove. I named each utensil, each pot and pan, and each food. Drew repeated the words, and after a few attempts was able to name most of them. Finally, I stood him on his feet. "You want to go back outside and play?"

He flicked his eyes toward the door, and I opened it. "John?" I called. "Come get Drew. Why don't you guys play something he can play?"

Several children scrambled out of the old army tent. "Let's play ring around the rosy," said one child.

I heard Marie behind me. "That's a baby game."

I looked at her. "You don't have to play."

"Good. I don't want to play baby games." Nevertheless, she ambled out the door and perched on the picnic table.

I went back to the kitchen, lit a cigarette and sank into the rocker. I laid my head back and listened to the kids.

"Ring around the rosy,
Pocket full of posies,
Ashes, ashes, all fall down!"

The last few words were accompanied by much giggling and I heard Dennis, a boy from down the block. "Drew, you're supposed to fall down. You can't just stand there."

The smell of frying potatoes filled the air as I heard the game start over again. I must have dozed, and I felt my cigarette burn my fingers. "Ouch," I said, and went to the sink. I extinguished the cigarette and let cold water run over my finger. As I stood there, the back door opened and the kids all trooped in. "Look, Mommy," John said. His black eyes sparkled. "Drew can do ring around the rosy."

The began their chant and moved around in a circle, hands linked. "All fall down!" they shouted, and I watched as John kicked Drew's feet out from under him.

I made an involuntary move toward Drew as he hit the floor. The other kids went down to. Drew giggled and didn't seem to be hurt as they all scrambled to their feet.

I turned to John. "What was that supposed to be?" I asked through clenched teeth.

"I hadda help Drew fall down. He won't fall down by himself when he's 'posed to." My oldest son was all innocence.

"We are supposed to be clear about what we want him to do. If you want him to fall down, you should press down on his shoulders when you're telling him to fall down. You do NOT kick his feet from under him. Do you understand?" I tried to keep my voice from rising and was only partially successful.

"Ok," John said, lower lip protruding slightly. "I was only helping him. You don't have to yell."

"I'm not yelling," I gritted. "Just go outside. And don't help him so hard next time."

. . .

With supper over and the dishwasher loaded, I took Drew by the hand. "Let's go fold laundry." John and Marie were settled in front of the television and I could hear the "Happy Days" theme. Gene was already situated in the recliner, his nose in a book.

I emptied a basket of freshly dried laundry onto my bed and began to fold them. "Towel," I said, and laid it in front of Drew.

He put his hand on it. "Towel," he said.

"Good!" I folded a pair of socks together and tossed them to him. He missed the catch, but picked them up.

"Socks," he said.

"Good talking!"

Fifteen minutes later, we were almost done folding the laundry and stowing it away when I heard Marie shouting something from the bathroom.

"Gene," I called. "Will you go see what Marie needs? I think she's in the bathtub." I put another stack of clothing in John's drawer, and heard Marie again. "Gene? Can you see what she wants?" I paused a moment and listened for his reply. Hearing nothing, I stomped into the hall and down to the bathroom.

I saw John try to push the door open and Marie tried to keep it from opening. Only John's knee kept her from closing it all the way. "I have to go to the bathroom, and she won't let me," John whined.

"Well, I was taking a bath first," Marie said, and shoved harder on the door.

"Ow, Mommy, she's breakin' my leg," John said, and held on to the door knob as if that were all that was keeping his leg from being broken off at the knee.

I pulled his hands off the knob and pushed the door open. Marie fell away from the door, clad only in a towel. "You seem to be finished. Let the water out and-- "

"But I--"

My head ached, my back was killing me, and I would have given anything for ten uninterrupted minutes. "Go on. The boys have still got to have a bath."

Marie looked at me, but said nothing as she flounced from the bathroom, wet hair streaming behind her.

When the tub had emptied, I rinsed it, then ran it half full of water and pulled John's clothes off. "Drew, come in here. Let's get you bathed."

He edged in from the hallway and looked at his brother, already surrounded by tub toys. "Bath," he said, and pointed.

"Good talking," I said.

When I had washed both children, I took Drew out first, wrapped him in a towel and took him to his room.

As I was dressing him for bed, I heard a thump from the bathroom, then a shrill cry.

I left Drew on the bed and raced back to the bathroom. John knelt on the floor with one hand to his bloody face. "Oh, my God, Son. What did you do?" I grabbed a clean wash cloth from the linen closet and wet it with cold water. I tried to clean the blood away, but it just kept coming.

"Gene!" I shouted. "Help me, will you?" From the corner of my eye, I saw both Marie and Drew at the bathroom door, wide-eyed and silent. "Marie, get Daddy."

She ran down the hall shrieking, "Daddy, Daddy. John's bleeding everywhere!"

I applied as much pressure as I dared, and the bleeding slowed enough that I could see the short but apparently very deep cut about an inch under his eye. "What happened? How did you do it?"

"I fell down," he sobbed.

"I know, Honey, but what did you cut it on?"

He pointed at an object near the floor, behind the door. It was the metal door stop, minus its rubber tip.

Gene appeared in the doorway. "Let me see." He removed the cloth for a second, then replaced it. "Looks like it's going to need some stitches," he said.

I groaned. "Oh, God. All right. Marie, get your brother some underwear, a pair of shorts and a shirt." Gene went to fetch the car around front, and we set off, en masse, to the emergency room. I leaned my forehead against the cool car window. "What next?" I wondered, and steeled myself for a long night.

Chapter 12

I awoke with a start and looked at the clock. It was almost eight and I had overslept. The long hours at the emergency room had taken their toll. I felt like I had been beaten. I swung my legs over the side of the bed and grabbed my robe, then dashed into the hall. "Kids, get up. We overslept." I ran into Marie's room and shook her. "Come on, Sis, you're going to be late. Get up."

She rolled over and yawned, then threw the sheet off her. Satisfied that she was on her way, I trotted over to the boys' bedroom. Drew stirred, but John lay so still, I thought he must still be asleep. As I got closer, though, I saw that his eyes were open. At least one of them was.

"Oh, my God, Son. Your poor face." His eye was almost closed from the swelling, and I reached out to touch the angry red lump on his face. It was fiery hot.

"It hurts, Mommy," he whispered.

"I know it does, Sweetie. I'm going to go call the doctor. You stay still." I ducked down to the lower bunk. "Drew, get up. Come on." He rolled over and sat up, and I left the room on the run.

I dialed the hospital with shaking fingers, and within minutes of my call, the doctor who had stitched John up called back.

"Sounds like an infection," he said. "You'd better bring him back in.

I called Gene and explained the situation. "Do you want me to come home?" he asked.

I hesitated. "Will you?" I lit my first cigarette of the day and held my breath, anticipating a negative answer.

"Sure I will. Just hang tight."

I cradled the phone, surprised but pleased in spite of the situation which had provoked this burst of husbandly help. Maybe there was life in our marriage yet.

I flew around the kitchen on wings of fear and managed a hasty breakfast of cinnamon toast and milk, then sent Marie off to school. By the time John and Drew were dressed, I could hear Gene in the driveway outside.

John fussed most of the way to the hospital. "I don't want stitches again, Mommy. Promise I won't, Ok?" He leaned against me and the heat from his body seemed intense.

"I can't promise, John. I don't think you will, but I don't know." I smoothed his dark hair back from his forehead.

At the hospital, the doctor "tsk-ed" and "hmm-ed" a great deal, but told us very little. Finally, he gave John a shot of antibiotics, which prompted a wail from the child.

"Did I forget to say I don't want no shots either?" he asked, as tears ran down his cheeks. He rubbed his leg where the needle had entered. "I don't like shots."

The doctor sent us home with a bottle of antibiotic liquid and assured me that the situation was now under control.

Two hours later, the wound had swollen even more and his temperature was up another degree. "I think you'd better bring him back in," the doctor told me.

I called Gene again, and he returned home, this time with a cousin in tow. Gayla would watch Drew and wait for Marie if we happened to be tied up for a long period of time.

By the time we reached the emergency room, John was deathly still, and the wound was a shiny, swollen purple mess. The doctor took one look and forgot to even "tsk."

He grabbed the nearest phone. "I want you to take him to Children's Hospital," he said, his voice strained.

When we reached Children's, a Dr. Speakman was waiting for us. He looked at John's face and let out a low whistle. "How long ago did this happen?"

"Last night," I said.

"That's pretty quick," he mused. "Well, we'll fix you up, fellow."

"No shots," John whispered.

I winced as I saw a nurse approach with an IV stand and tray. I looked at Gene's pale face, and he turned away as the doctor prepared to insert the IV shunt.

"We're going to use the scattergun approach for now," he said. "We don't know what bacteria is causing this, so we'll give him a variety of antibiotics."

John moaned. "Is this a shot?"

A nurse patted his arm and directed his attention away from the doctor. She spoke to him in a soft voice and his face relaxed.

The doctor glanced at John, then continued. "When the lab tests are done, we will have isolated what the bacteria is, and treat it accordingly." He slapped tape over the shunt and straightened up. "We'll move him up to an isolation ward shortly." He patted my hand. "There'll be a cot in there so one of you can stay with him," he said.

I sank into a chair beside the gurney on which John lay. His face seemed vividly colored against the sheet, and his black eyes were shadowed.

Suddenly, I shot up from the chair. "Oh, my God, Gene. What time is it?"

He glanced at his watch. "Quarter till one. Why?"

I rummaged through my purse. "I've got to call Ivar and Andi. They'll think no telling what."

"Oh, for Christ's sake, Julia. Can't you let it go one time?" He turned away and jammed his hands into his trouser pockets.

"No, I can't. Have you got a dime? All I have are pennies." I looked at him as if daring him to refuse me.

With a disgusted sigh, he flipped a coin at me. I hurried down the hall to a pay phone and called the clinic.

The secretary put me right through. "Thank God, Julia!" Ivar's voice boomed through the receiver. "We did not know what became of you. Howard has been on needles and pins."

I explained as quickly as I could about John's accident and subsequent infection. "So Gene and I are up here with him for I'm not sure how long."

"Fine, fine. It is where you should be," Ivar agreed. "I think, though, that the team should continue to come to Reseda and work with Drew. We do not want to disrupt his routine any more than necessary." He paused. "And we do not want to lose what progress he has made."

My heart sank. "I don't know how long I'll be here, and I don't think Gene--"

"Not to worry, Julia. We have managed very well thus far and will continue to do so. He is welcome to take part, but I will not force the issue with your husband."

I sighed in relief. "Thank you, Ivar."

"Not at all, not at all," he said, and I could clearly picture his magnanimous wave.

Tears threatened to choke me and I hung up in haste. I dug for a tissue in my purse. Ivar and Andi and Howard--all the members of Drew's therapy team-- had become so incredibly dear to me. I blew my nose and tried to stem the flow of tears. How could I ever thank them enough for their kindness and hard work?

I went back down the hall to the cubicle John lay in. Gene stood at the room's lone window staring out, and turned as I entered. "Get everything worked out?"

I nodded and sank down into the vinyl chair beside John's gurney. "They're going to go ahead and go to the house and work with Drew." I smoothed John's hair back from his clammy forehead.

"Hm," Gene said. He came and stood beside the bed and looked down at John, but spoke to me. "I think I'd better go let Gayla know what's going on, and call Mom and Dad. Maybe they can come down and stay with the kids till this is over."

I nodded, distracted. "Whatever you think," I said, glad to be able to leave it in his hands.

Gene patted me on the shoulder. "I'll be back," he said. He turned to go toward the door, and I called to him.

"Gene? When your folks get to Reseda, can you bring my car up? I need to be able to come home to shower and change."

"I will if Dad can follow me up here. I'll have to ask him."

"Sure." I returned his wave, and he was gone.

. . .

Once John was moved to an isolation area, all visitors had to scrub upon entering and leaving the room. I sat at John's bedside the remainder of the day, leaving only to smoke an occasional cigarette. Each time I rose to leave, John's voice stopped me at the door.

"Don't leave, Mommy."

"I won't. I'm going to smoke a cigarette down the hall. I'll be back in just a few minutes, okay?"

"Okay," he would nod, satisfied until my next exit.

The floor we were on was a busy one, and, as evening fell, I looked up every time footsteps neared the doorway. I expected Gene to return, but by 10 p.m., I realized he wasn't going to re-appear, at least not that evening.

I left the room one last time at 10:30. I trudged down the hallway to the pay phone, weary beyond belief. Gene answered on the fourth ring.

I dispensed with the small talk. "Are you coming up tomorrow?"

I heard the snick of his lighter, then a deep inhale and exhale. "Yeah. I don't know when, though," he said.

"Well, bring my car. I need to see Drew and Marie, and take a shower. You can stay here with John while I'm gone can't you? It will only take a couple of hours."

"I don't know. I probably can."

"Probably? Look, Gene, I can't--"

"No, Julia, you look. I just don't know right now what my schedule is like, how long I can be up there. Just don't give me a hard time, all right?" His voice grew angry. "I gotta go. I was almost asleep when you called." With that, he hung up.

I stood with the receiver still to my ear and seethed. Of all the self-centered, uncaring--I jerked myself out of the whirlpool of anger I was in, and took a deep breath. "Okay," I said to myself. "We'll get through this just fine. John will get better, and everything will be fine." I only half believed it, but I knew challenging Gene right now would serve no purpose. When I lay down on the hard cot provided for me, I resolved to tough the situation with Gene out for now, and afterward--afterward, things were going to change. Of that I was certain.

. . .

John remained in Children's Hospital for five days, during which time none of Gene's visits lasted more than an hour. He didn't bring my car, and, since his car was owned by the government, there was no question of me driving it. His only concession to me was to bring cigarettes.

His behavior baffled me, but I finally crested the hill of disenchantment that signalled the end of my marriage. The dissolution of any union is unpleasant, but I was passed hurting. I maintained a stoic silence in

Gene's presence, speaking only when spoken to, and reminded myself over and over that when Drew finished therapy, I would take the children and move back to Oklahoma.

After the first day of John's hospitalization, when I realized that Gene had no intention of relieving me so I could go home and clean up, I took bitter pleasure in visiting a shop near Children's Hospital and purchasing, on our credit card, a new outfit each day. When the bills came in, after John was home, Gene paid them without comment.

. . .

I called Ivar's office on a daily basis to receive updates on Drew's work with the team, but the combined pressures of John's slow recovery and Gene's refusal to relieve me occasionally prevented me from really absorbing the information I received during the calls. Being away from Drew at that time could have been detrimental to his progress, but thanks to the dedication of Ivar and the therapy team, he came through with flying colors.

I threw myself back into Drew's treatment, praying that Gene and I could maintain the status quo until Drew was through with therapy. We maintained the illusion of a marriage, but the reality, for me, was cold and lonely. I had confided in no one about leaving Gene and California. Even Gene and I had not discussed it. I had no doubt that it was over, and knew that he didn't either.

. . .

After completing our first therapy session at UCLA after John's release from the hospital, I was exhausted.

By the time we picked up John at the daycare center and got home, it was nearly three. I started dinner while John played in the back yard in the old army tent Gene had set up for him. As I peeled potatoes, I watched him dart in and out of the tent and imagined the day when Drew would willingly accompany his brother on all the imaginary adventures little boys go on. So far, he only played with the other children if one of them took his hand and physically led him along.

Now, he squatted on the floor and emptied out a plastic container of multi-colored wooden circles and squares. Gene had spent most of the previous weekend making them, but as far as I could see, it was only an isolated burst of enthusiasm and heralded no major change in our relationship or of his attitude toward Drew's treatment.

I held up a potato in Drew's direction. "Look, Drew. A potato." He looked up, but chose not to answer. He turned back to his wooden toys.

As I put the potatoes on to fry, I heard a noise at the front door, ran to let Gene in, and then back to the kitchen.

When he had changed clothes, he came in and poured a glass of tea. Without comment he stepped around Drew on his way to and from the refrigerator, then sat down at the table and lit a cigarette. "I've got a surprise for you," he said.

I turned from the stove and looked to where he sat, encircled by a wreath of smoke. "A surprise?" Suspicion crept into my voice, but he seemed not to notice.

"Yeah, a surprise. What do you say to a week of fishing? Just you, me, and the kids." A grin turned up the corners of his mouth, but didn't seem to reach his eyes. They measured and appraised with seemingly calculated shrewdness.

I stood speechless, the greasy spatula still in one hand and the lid to the skillet in the other. Gene picked a piece of tobacco from his lower lip. "You don't like the idea?" he asked.

I finally found my voice, and the words sputtered out of me like the hot grease in the skillet. "Are you crazy? There's no way we can go anywhere right now. Drew's just starting to show some real progress." I turned back to the range.

"Oh, for Christ's sake, Julia. We can pick up where we leave off when we get back."

Shaking with barely suppressed fury, I slapped the lid back on the sputtering potatoes and turned to face Gene. "No, 'we' can't pick up where 'we' leave off," I snapped. "In the first place, it's not that easy, and in the second place, 'we' doesn't enter into it. You haven't done a damn thing since we started, except try to figure out ways to stop it." I lit a cigarette and blew out an angry plume of smoke.

"Don't be ridiculous," he said. "Who do you think made those things he's playing with right now? Did one of your stupid therapists sneak in--in the middle of the night--and make them or what?"

"Stupid? Is that what you think? This therapy is stupid?" My voice became more shrill and I knew I should shut up, but the words kept coming as if a powerful force pushed them out of my mouth. I slammed down the spatula. "I'll tell you what's stupid, Gene. Stupid is denying there's anything wrong with Drew. Stupid is refusing to attend his therapy sessions because you're too important to carry a sack lunch. Stupid is going to San Diego every weekend instead of doing the things that need doing around here. Stupid is leaving me stuck at Children's Hospital for five days. That's what stupid is!" I inhaled deeply and tried to calm myself, but instead, I felt close to tears.

He sat motionless for a moment, then deliberately ground his cigarette out in the plastic ashtray in front of him. "I'm going, with or without you."

It sounded like a threat, and served only to increase my anger. "Fine," I shot back. "You haven't included us in your life in a long time, anyway. Why start now?"

Gene's face looked hard and unrelenting. "Is that the way you feel, Julia?" His eyes bore into mine.

I dropped my gaze to the floor. I wanted to jump up and down and scream, but I didn't. The silence was broken only by the sounds of Drew clacking the wooden circles and squares together.

That night, as I lay beside Gene in the darkness of our room, I felt an overwhelming fear of the path a divorce would set me on. It wasn't too late to humble myself before Gene and patch the tattered remains of our marriage. Should I, and just accept this life as my only choice? If not, could I take care of my children alone? Was I strong enough to endure the life of a single mother? The prospect seemed so frightening to me. I put a hand on my husband's shoulder.

"Gene, I--"

He shook my hand away. "Go to sleep, Julia."

Stung, I turned my back to him and huddled on the edge of the bed, an occasional tear running sideways across my face. The abstract price I had been willing to pay when Drew first began therapy had become concrete. Now that it had, was I still willing?

. . .

No more was said about a family fishing trip, but I could see more clearly than ever the shambles my marriage lay in. Nothing emphasized those ruins more than the sight of Gene as he drove off into the early morning gloom, his car loaded with fishing gear and camping equipment. "Pretty strange behavior for a guy who wanted a houseful of kids," I said as I watched the car's tail lights wink out of sight. I sighed and lit a cigarette.

I woke the children and fed them breakfast, determined to keep everything as normal as possible for them. As I straightened the kitchen afterward, I looked at the clock.

"Oops," I said to Drew, as usual the last one to leave the table. "You'd better hurry, Son. Andi's going to be here soon."

He put a last spoonful of cereal in his mouth, then slid down from his chair and came across the room to me. Holding his arms over his head, he said, "Off."

I smiled and pulled his pajama top slowly over his head, and paused for a moment when it covered his face. "Where's Drew?" I asked, then pulled the top off. "Oh, there he is!"

His gaze didn't meet mine, but a sly smile tugged at the corners of his mouth before he ran from the kitchen and down the hallway to his bedroom. I smiled, amazed at the pleasure I derived from such a simple act, and went to dress him.

Andi and Laurie arrived promptly at eleven. "Hi," Andi said. She tweaked John's belly. "How goes it with you, Munchkin?"

John reddened with evident pleasure. "Want to see my picture I made my Mommy?" he asked, and pulled Andi into the kitchen. I heard her oohs and ahs as she viewed the picture where it hung on the wall over the table.

When they re-entered the room, Drew edged in from the hallway. He didn't look at Andi or John, but his sly smile showed his awareness of their presence.

John still hung onto Andi's hand with both of his, and chattered to her about pre-school and a particularly noteworthy turtle he had captured in the back yard the day before.

Andi held her other hand out to Drew. "Hey, Munchkin. Come here."

The tip of Drew's tongue showed outside one corner of his mouth, as if in an effort to comply, but he walked to the other side of the room, away from his brother and Andi. Fearing that John's proximity to Andi might be a source of distraction to Drew, I held out my hand. "John, come over here with me."

Disappointment clouded his face, but he came. Laurie pulled a semi-reluctant Drew across the room and she and Andi began a play-tug-of-war with him. Andi sat down on the floor, and pulled Drew down with her. She said something to Laurie, and Laurie dug in her enormous leather-fringed handbag. Soon she extracted two square, beige containers, one larger than the other.

John tapped my leg and motioned me down toward him. "I want to tell you something," he said.

I put my head next to his. He cut his eyes toward Drew, Andi, and Laurie, and whispered, "I want to play, too."

I squatted beside him, and noticed Andi looking at us, her forehead wrinkled slightly. "Honey, they're not really playing. This is Drew's therapy."

He looked at the group with doubtful eyes. "They look like they're playing," he said. "They're having fun."

I sighed. "I know, but they're--"

Andi's voice interrupted me. "John, why don't you come and help us."

His face lit up, and he glanced at me. "Can I?"

"Oh, Andi, I don't know, I mean--"

She held up her hand. "A family affair, remember?"

I hesitated, then gave John a little push. "All right. Go on."

I sat back on the couch and lit a cigarette as I watched. Marie wandered in from outside, two friends tagging behind. They glanced at the group on the floor.

"What are they doing?" one of them asked.

Marie waved her hand. "They're just teaching my brother stuff. He's autistic," she said, as if explaining left-handedness. Her friends seemed impressed, and followed her down the hall toward her bedroom.

"Julia, I need a--well, anything that will fit into these containers," Andi said.

One of Drew's toy cars lay on the end table beside me. I picked it up and tossed it to her. "Try this."

She caught it. "OK, John. Here's the deal. We're going to help Drew learn about 'in' and 'on,' right?"

John nodded, his face solemn. "Right," he echoed.

"OK, you take the car. When I say 'in,' drop it into the cup."

"Drew. Look!" she said, her voice loud. "Goo-ood, good looking!" she enthused. "Drew. In," she said, and John dropped the car into the container.

After a few seconds, Laurie removed the car and handed it back to John. "In," Andi said again. John repeated the action. This time, Andi removed the car, and handed it to John. "OK, John, let's let Drew do it this time. Give him the car."

John attempted to give Drew the car, put Drew sat passively, unwilling to take the toy.

After John had tried several times unsuccessfully, Laurie held her hand out. "Let me see it, John," she said. She took it and put it in Drew's hand, with the words, "Drew take car!" She closed his hand on it and said, "Goo-ood!"

When she released Drew's hand, he dropped the car. "No!" she said, and closed his fingers around it again. "Drew take car!" When she released his hand this time, he held onto the toy. "Go-ood," she and Andi said together. John looked from one woman to the other, then added his own voice. "Go-ood, Drew," he said, in such perfect imitation that we all laughed.

By the end of the session, I had joined in, and we were all exhausted, but Drew now followed instructions to put the car in and on the containers more often than not.

When we released him, he grabbed his car and ran across the room, where he stood spinning the car's wheels. He seemed to be ignoring us, but his sly grin told me otherwise. My amazement at the change in him grew with each session, but I was still not ready for Andi's next announcement.

"Another month or so, and I think he'll be about ready," she said, and flipped her dark hair behind her.

I halted in the middle of grinding my cigarette out.
"Ready for what?" I asked.
"Pre-school," she said.

Chapter 13

Preschool!" I gasped. "You're joking. Surely not so soon." The idea of Drew going anywhere without me brought forth images of disaster that no third-world earthquake could match. It wasn't that he was destructive, but the single-minded determination of the autistic child could put him in potentially hazardous situations. How could any normal child care center watch him carefully enough?

Andi laughed. "You act like I suggested he go on a cross-country trip alone. It's just pre-school, just for a few hours at a time. He needs the interaction with others. And he won't be alone, not at first." She squeezed my shoulder. "I bet Drew will do great."

"He's made progress, but what if he has a setback or something?"

"C'mon, Julia, we wouldn't let him go if we thought any harm would come to him."

"I don't know. . ." I said, and my voice trailed off as I watched John attempt to get Drew to roll the car toward him. Drew turned his face from his brother and looked toward the opposite wall with unseeing eyes. Interaction, I thought. Yeah. Right. I saw improvement in Drew, but not that much. Still, I did not want to lose one iota of the progress we had made.

The look on my face must have spoken volumes. Andi squeezed my shoulders again. "Look, we won't be starting with pre-school. First, we'd like you to scope out some kind of activity that the two of you can do together, and when he makes it through that, we'll talk about preschool again." She sighed. "Julia, we have to be careful not to lose sight of the goal of therapy--to help Drew live a normal life. That means contact with others, going places and doing things. He's got to broaden his horizons, and it's up to us to help him do it."

"I know."

Andi dropped her hand, and pulled her hair back behind her shoulder. "Well, we need to all be thinking of some ways for peer contact, some structured interaction. He needs exposure to different people and places. Think about it tonight, and we'll talk tomorrow." She hesitated a moment, then grinned. "And remember, we haven't lost a mother yet."

After they left, I roamed restlessly through the house. Committed as I was to Drew's eventual recovery, I still had not given much thought to his future. Now, the more I thought about what Andi had said, the more it made sense. He did need to spend time with other children, besides John and Marie and the occasional neighborhood child. They all seemed to have become accustomed to his little idiosyncrasies and perhaps they offered little in the way of challenges for him to meet and adapt to. But what could I do?

. . .

"Hey, Mom, I'm home." Marie bounded into the house, and sped down the hallway toward her room. I followed, and glanced into the boys' room on the way.

Drew sat on the floor, engrossed in play, several small trucks and cars spread out before him.

In her room, I watched as Marie tossed a handful of papers onto the bed. I picked them up and flipped through them. I stopped at one with a big, red A on it. "Hey, this is great."

She came to me and looked at the paper. "Oh. Well, the test wasn't that hard," she said. She took the papers from me and shuffled through them herself. "There's one in here I was supposed to give you." She went through them a second time, and finally found the one she was looking for. "Here."

I looked at the *Cantara Street School News*. I always enjoyed reading the newsletter, and tried to keep up with what went on in Marie's school. I took it into the kitchen and sat at the table with a cigarette. An item near the bottom of the page caught my attention.

"Mommy And Me Classes will be offered one day a week for parents and preschoolers," it said. I thought about it for a moment, then went to the phone. I called the number listed on the sheet and a secretary at the school gave me the needed information. As I thought about the possibilities it would offer, I went to the window to check on John. He and Terry, a neighborhood boy moved into and out of the old army tent, chasing each other. Suddenly, John broke away and ran to the house.

"Mommy," he shouted as he banged in the back door. "We're thirsty." His high color and damp hair testified to the fact. He came to me and wrapped both arms around my legs. With his sweaty little body pressed against me, he made a face and said, "I'm strong, huh, Mommy? I'm the Incredible Hulk," he said.

He released me and held his arms up in a menacing gesture. "Gr-r-r," he said.

I laughed. "You're incredible, all right. And if you'll move, I'll get you something to drink." John ran back out the door, and I saw him re-join Terry, motioning toward the house.

As I mixed up a powdered soft drink, I was suddenly seized by inspiration. I stood still for a moment, then grabbed a plate and a bag of cookies from the cabinet. I put the cookies on the plate, tucked some paper cups under one arm, and went to the living room door.

"Drew. You want some cookies?"

He appeared at the other end of the living room, almost as if by magic, a small grin on his face.

I motioned with my head toward the back door. "Come on, we'll have them outside." He came toward me, and I handed him the paper cups. "You carry these, and I'll get the drinks."

In the backyard, John and Terry bounded up to the picnic table. Drew hung back only a little. "Do you guys want some cookies to go with your drinks?" I asked.

"Yeah," they chorused. "Cookies."

As they seated themselves at the wooden table, Terry grabbed a cookie and pulled it apart to eat the creamy middle. "My mom never lets me have cookies now. She makes me wait till after supper," he said.

"Is that right? Well, we're going to have cookies here every afternoon. Maybe a little earlier than this," I said. "If you have any other friends around here, tell them they can come, too, if it's all right with their mothers."

I sat Drew down among them, cookies and a paper cup full of red liquid in front of him. He glanced at the two other boys, briefly, then at his cookies. Finally, he picked up one sandwich cookie, pulled it open, and began to eat the creme filling.

"Little late to be passing that junk out, isn't it, Julia?"

I jumped. "Oh, Gene. You scared the life out of me."

John turned to look up at this father. "Hi, Daddy."

Gene ruffled John's hair, but looked at me. "Can you leave the kids and come in? I've got something I want to talk to you about."

I hesitated. "Can it wait? I'd kind of like to hang around out here."

"Oh, come on. The gate's locked, and you can watch them through the window if it's that important."

"Well, all right," I said, and turned to John. "Watch your brother, OK?"

John nodded, and took another cookie from the plate. I followed Gene into the house, curious as to what could be so important.

He went to the refrigerator, and poured a glass of tea. Going to the table, he sat down and lit a cigarette. "I've taken a part-time job," he said.

"You have? Where?"

"Sears."

"Won't that cut into your fishing time?" I asked.

He shook his head. "No. I'll still have weekends free."

Well, bully for you, I thought. The man didn't recognize sarcasm when he heard it. "Why are you doing this now?"

He shrugged. "I thought we could use the extra money. We can't expect your parents to foot the bill for John's pre- school forever."

I lit a cigarette. "I guess not. And Drew will be starting sometime soon."

"Really? Well, that's great," he said, with more enthusiasm than I had heard in his voice since the therapy began.

"Yeah. Great," I echoed, a knot of worry still heavy in my mid-section. I remembered the Mommy and Me classes. "As a prelude to preschool, I think I've found another activity for him. For him and me, actually."

"What's that?" Gene went to the refrigerator and poured another glass of tea.

I ran water over my cigarette and put it into the waste can. "Well, it's called 'Mommy and Me,' and it's on Thursday mornings at the school. They'll have activities for the kids, and a discussion group for the mothers, then everybody has lunch together."

"Oh."

I could tell his mind was already somewhere else. I sighed and lit another cigarette.

The next day at Dr. Lovaas' offices, I mentioned the *Mommy and Me* program.

"That would be ideal," Dr. Lovaas said. "But that is one day a week, is it not?"

I nodded. "But I've come up with a way to keep kids around the house more. If their mothers don't lynch me." I explained my bribery of the previous afternoon. "They probably have a hard enough time getting the kids to eat nutritional foods without me filling them up with junk food." I saw Laurie, Howard and Andi exchange looks, and knew they thought I made too big a deal out of a few cookies. Someday, I thought, you'll have kids and worry about the same piddling things.

"Sounds great to me," Andi said. "Maybe you could do it a little earlier in the day."

I nodded. "Sure. I just didn't think of it yesterday until late."

Andi stood. "OK, guys, let's get down to business."

Howard, Laurie, and I stood, and I lit a cigarette. As I blew the smoke out, I asked, "What are we going to work on today?"

Andi thought for a moment, and said, "I think I'd like to build a new skill using colors and shapes next. As soon as he gets that down, we'll start on 'first' and 'last.'" She paused a moment. "We might as well pick out some small items that Drew knows the names of, for when we do the 'first' and 'last' task."

"How about car?" Laurie volunteered.

"OK," Andi said. "We can use one of his little cars. What else?" Her eyes searched the room and a little crease appeared in her forehead.

"What about cookie? Or shirt?" I offered.

Andi shook her head. "He'd eat the cookie, and 'shirt' is too big."

Laurie clapped her hands. "I know--how about 'clip?' He knows what a paper clip is."

"Oh, yeah. That's a good one," Howard said.

I thought hard for a moment. "How about 'key?'" I asked, and pointed to my keys where they lay on the table.

"That's good," Laurie and Howard said in unison, but Andi shook her head.

"No. 'Key' won't work. It's too close to 'clip.' We need another word with more auditory discrimination."

I frowned. "But clip and car are close, too."

"Yes, but he knows for certain what car is, and clip is just one more thing. Put key in there, and it's two more things. That creates an extra problem we don't want to get into right now."

I lit another cigarette, and pondered her words for a few moments. "All right. I think I see." I paused, then said, "What about fork and spoon? He knows the word for fork, but I'm not sure about spoon. And maybe TV Guide?"

"That's a good one. And spoon and fork will be good, too. OK. Today, we'll do colors and shapes, and we'll make sure he knows clip and spoon. Let's put off teaching 'first' and 'last' until tomorrow." She pulled her hair back and finger-combed it. "Let's get to it."

We worked on colors and shapes, which Drew picked up easily, then for the rest of the session we taught Drew to point to the spoon and clip when requested to do so.

The next morning, the session was at home and Andi began by reviewing colors and shapes. She dumped several plastic, brightly colored shapes onto the floor, along with a wooden piece that stood upright.

"See," she said, and pulled her hair over her shoulder to get it out of the way. "He puts the shapes onto this wooden thing. I think he's far enough along that the hole in the middle of the shapes won't throw him off."

I nodded. "Probably."

"Drew. Come on, Munchkin. Time to go to work."
She extended her hand to him, and he came across the
room to her. "Sit down here with me."

He sat, legs extended, and Andi crossed them for
him, Indian style. He picked up a yellow circle and
examined it, put it down and picked up a red square.

Andi took it from him and put it on the floor. She
removed all the shapes except a red circle, a red square,
and a red triangle. "Touch red circle," she said.

Drew touched the red circle.

"Good boy," Andi said. She gave him a tiny piece of
cookie, then tickled him. "You're a good kid, you know
that?" He giggled. She released him and arranged
another series of shapes, this time in blue. "Touch blue
square."

He did. She popped a piece of cookie into his
mouth, and patted his arm. "Goo-od deal. You touched
blue square. Touch blue triangle."

Andi went through yellow shapes, purple ones,
orange and green ones. Then she placed three circles,
each a different color, on the floor. "Touch red circle."

I held my breath. Could he do this? Would he
remember, or was the task too complicated?

Drew hesitated a moment. His hand went toward
the blue circle, and I fought the urge to cry out to him.
Finally, his hand went to the red circle and he touched
it.

"All right! Go-ood job, Drew. What a good worker
you are," Andi said, and put another piece of cookie in
his mouth. He received it with a delighted smile, and I
released my breath, surprised to feel tears spring to my
eyes. I wiped them away, and hoped no one noticed.

"Why don't we stop for a play-break," Andi said
after praising Drew lavishly. We went to the back yard

and played with Drew and John for a short time, pushing them in the swings, and watching daredevil John's dives from the picnic table.

After our play-break, we all straggled in from outside. "Now what?" Howard asked.

"Let's start on 'first' and 'last,'" Andi said. Before beginning the task, she tested Drew's knowledge of the spoon and clip. When she was satisfied that he recognized the two items, and knew what they were called, she began.

She placed one of Drew's small cars in front of him. "First," she said. She then placed an issue of TV Guide in front of him. "Last." She paused a moment, then said, "Touch first." She took Drew's hand and laid it on the car. "Goo-ood," she said. "You touched first. Now, touch last." She placed his hand on the TV Guide. "Goo-ood," she said. "You touched last."

Now, Andi picked up the fork and discarded the car. She laid the fork down and said, "First," and laid the TV guide down again and said, "Last." She paused a moment, and said, "Touch first." She placed his hand on the fork, then praised him and gave him a tiny piece of cookie. She explained. "We need to switch items each time, so he won't think we're trying to teach him another name for the same item."

Within an hour, Drew consistently pointed to the correct objects. "Drew, I think you've got it," Andi said. "Now, let's see if you can do one more thing." She laid the clip on the floor in front of Drew and said, "First," then she laid the TV Guide in front of him and said, "Last." She paused a moment. "Touch first."

Drew touched the clip. "Goo-ood," Andi said, and patted his arm. She pointed to the clip. "What's this?" she asked in her normal tone of voice, then leaned close and whispered something in his ear.

"First," Drew said.

We all applauded, with cheers of "Good job, Drew!" Andi repeated the discrete trial several times, and Drew performed correctly every time.

After one last trial, Andi grabbed Drew and tickled, then hugged him. A broad grin lit his face. He clearly enjoyed Andi's attentions. The changes in him became more apparent each day. I silently thanked God and prayed for continued progress.

Chapter 14

EXCERPT FROM THERAPY LOG

April 10

Home:
Drew was in excellent spirits. Seemed very excited to see us, smiled and laughed when we came in. Worked on labeling some new things. He learned several new words including man, sandwich, couch. Drew is talking a great deal, repeating things that are said to him, and naming people and objects.

April 11
UCLA:
Videotaped
Began new way of working on pronouns. "Touch Drew's nose. Whose nose? My nose." "Touch Andi's nose. Whose nose? Your nose." Drew picked up on "my nose, my head," etc. very fast.

As Drew improved, my marriage continued it's slow decline. The "Mommy and Me" classes and therapy became my only source of contact with other adults, but I felt no real unhappiness. Gene was home very seldom, and when he was, the tense silence seemed to keep everyone so on edge it seemed a relief to have him gone.

Therapy continued, becoming more and more exciting to me as Drew improved. In April, Andi announced that it was time to begin working on pronouns.

"Pronouns?" I asked.

She flopped down on the white leather couch and nodded. "It's a difficult concept for autistics to grasp."

"Why should it be?" I asked. "It's just more words, isn't it?"

Andi shook her dark head and smoothed her hair back. "No, not really. We learn from what people say to us." She thought for a moment. "For instance, we might say, 'Drew, do you want a cookie?' A typically autistic answer might be, 'Yes, you want a cookie.' He might think from the way we talk to him that he is supposed to use 'you', or 'yours', instead of 'I', 'me' and 'my'."

"I see. I never thought of it that way, but I can understand the difficulty." The concept of language and how children learn it intrigued me. Though I told no one at the time, I began to consider going back to college for a degree of my own. I didn't know what field, exactly, but I knew it would involve children.

Andi slapped her knees and stood. "Ok, guys, let's get to work." She held out a hand to Drew, who squatted on the floor nearby with a fleet of small cars. He ignored her for a moment, and my stomach tightened.

"Drew!" she said, more sharply this time.

Only when he looked up and grinned did my stomach muscles relax. Will the fear of regression never leave me? I wondered. I could only hope that as Drew continued to do well, it would.

He came to Andi, a blue car in his hand. He held it toward her. "Blue car!" he exclaimed, as if it was the first he had ever seen.

Andi laughed and ruffled his hair. "Good going, Drew!" She pulled him to the center of the room and sat down with her legs crossed, yoga style. She patted the floor in front of her. "Come on."

Drew sat. Andi took the car from him and put it to the side. "Touch Drew's nose."

Drew responded correctly. Andi ran him through several trials in which he touched his own nose. He seemed to fully understand the instruction. She changed it.

"Touch Andi's nose," she said.

He reached out and touched her nose with a forefinger, and giggled.

"Good touching, Drew," she said. For several more trials, she told him to "Touch Andi's nose."

When he seemed to thoroughly understand the command, Andi changed it once again. "Touch YOUR Drew's nose," she said, and emphasized the word "your." She brought his hand to his nose again, and his head bobbed slightly. "Touch YOUR Drew's nose," she repeated.

Drew's dark eyes clouded a little, and he hesitated, then touched Andi's nose. "Andi's nose," he said.

"No!" Andi said, a sharp edge to her voice. "Touch YOUR Drew's nose," she said, and prompted him by moving his hand to his own nose.

His attention seemed to waver, and he glanced at me. "Shee-shee," he said, indicating that he needed to go to the bathroom.

I shepherded him to the bathroom and back. "I guess he didn't really have to go," I said. Andi nodded. "He just doesn't like this." She raised his hand to his nose, and said, "Touch Drew's YOUR nose. Go- ood, you touched Drew's YOUR nose." She gave him the same instructions several times before she quit prompting him. "Touch Drew's YOUR nose. Touch Drew's YOUR nose," she said.

Drew stared at Andi, his bottom lip caught in his teeth. The room became silent except for the "blub-blub of the water cooler.

I sat as still as I could, as if to move would break the cocoon of concentration Drew and Andi were caught in. Slowly, Drew stretched his arm out, then dropped it and looked at me. "Shee-shee?"

I glanced at Andi, and she gave an almost imperceptible nod of her head. I took him once more to the bathroom, and once again, he failed to urinate.

He sat down in front of Andi once more and she took his hand and placed it on his nose. After a few more trials, Andi waved me over. "Come on, your turn." She got to her feet and stretched, and I took her place.

"Touch Drew's YOUR nose," I said, and moved his hand to his nose. "Good deal. You touched Drew's YOUR nose." I brought his hand to his nose again. "Touch Drew's YOUR nose," I said. "Good. You touched Drew's YOUR nose."

"Julia," Andi said, "Try fading the prompt now."

"Okay." I brought Drew's hand to his nose. "Touch Drew's YOUR nose," I said, and lowered my voice slightly when I pronounced Drew's name. Over the next few trials, I said it more and more softly, until I said only, "Touch your nose."

Finally, Drew moved his hand to his nose himself, touched it and repeated, "Touch your nose."

"Good touching, Drew!" I said.

"Way to go, Drew," said Howard from the doorway he had just entered.

Andi got down on her knees and tickled Drew. "All right, Munchkin!" she said. "Way to be." Drew giggled and fell onto his back. Andi pulled him up and onto her lap. "Good work! Now, we need to have some fun." She looked at me. "Tomorrow's Saturday. You want to take the kids to the zoo?"

I poked Drew in the tummy. "How about it? You want to go to the zoo?"

"The zoo," he repeated, and poked his own belly, then giggled at his joke.

"The zoo it is," I said.

. . .

The sprawling Los Angeles Zoo teemed with children. Drew stared open-mouthed at them as well as the animals. John and Tina ran ahead, then back, to Laurie, Andi, Howard and I, but Drew stuck close.

"Mom, I want to see the monkeys and the hoppopitamus," John said.

"Hippopotamus," Marie said in her recently-acquired big-sister-knows-it-all-voice. "You mean hippopotamus."

John gave her a look of disgust. "That's what I said." He turned to me. "Can we? Now?"

"We'll get to them eventually," I said. "Let's just take it as it comes, all right?"

"Look, guys, there's the petting zoo," Andi said. "Why don't we go over there? You want to, Drew?" She held her hand out to him, and he took it.

"But, Mom, I want to see the--" John began.

"The hoopapootamus," Marie teased.

John ignored her. "Mom, please--"

"Both of you stop it," I said, and lit a cigarette. "Come on. We'll go to the petting zoo now and see the monkeys and hippos when we get to them." I took John's hand and walked toward the petting zoo.

"Hippopoota-mouse," I heard Marie say behind me.

John pulled on my hand. "Marie's making whispers at me. Make her stop it."

"Both of you had better cease and desist right now. I don't want to hear it." We entered the gate to the petting zoo. I saw Drew and Andi across the lot. Drew had a head lock on a pygmy goat, a blissful smile on his face, if not the goat's.

"Aw, look, Julia," Howard said behind me.

I turned to see a lamb, wooly and white, standing on unsteady legs. "How sweet," I said. I stroked the lamb's soft wool. "Look, John. I don't think you've ever seen a lamb up close before."

An attendant held a baby bottle out. "Would you like to feed her?" she asked.

"Yeah!" John said. He took the bottle and held it out to the lamb, who knew exactly what to do with it. It sucked so vigorously that John had a difficult time holding onto the bottle.

"Hey, guy, let me help," Howard said. He squatted beside John and helped hold the bottle.

I stood and smoked for a few moments, then turned to see where Drew and Marie were. Marie stood near a small pen talking to an attendant and stroking another goat. She saw me and waved. I waved back and went to where Drew and Andi stood.

Drew looked up. "Mommy. Drew feed." He patted the goat next to him. "Drew feed."

"Does it take a bottle, too?" I asked Andi.

She shook her head. "No, but you can put money in that machine over there." She pointed across the lot. "It dispenses some kind of feed."

"Okay." I dug through the mess in my purse and found both bills and change. I went to the machine and returned with a small plastic bag full of pellet-like things.

"Don't spill them," I said, as I opened the package and gave it to Drew.

"Don't spill them," he echoed.

"No! No bad talking," Andi said automatically. Drew was at all times discouraged from echolalia, a compulsive repetition of words spoken by another person, including the other speakers' tone and accent.

Drew picked out one pellet and held it out to the goat. When the goat reached for it with his mouth and touched Drew's hand, Drew jerked back and dropped the pellet.

Andi squatted beside him. "It's okay. He won't hurt you." She poured some feed into her hand. "Do this," she said, and held the pellets out on her flat palm. The goat took them, then nudged her gently for more.

Drew poured a few into his own hand and held them out. The goat picked them up gently as if he knew he had a novice goat feeder before him. Drew giggled. "Drew feed him," he said.

When the feed was gone, Drew held out his hands. "Feed him some more."

I laughed. "All right, come on. Let's go get some more."

After three more trips to the vending machine, Drew still wanted to feed the goat. "Some more, Mommy," he begged. "Feed him some more."

I looked at Andi. "Do you think it will hurt the goat?"

She shrugged. "I guess it'll quit eating when it gets full. One more bag probably won't hurt. They're small."

At that moment, the goat let loose a stream of urine. A startled look came over Drew, then he squatted to look under the animal. "Shee-shee, Mommy." He pointed. "Shee- shee."

"Boy, I'll say," I laughed. I dug through my purse and a couple of bills fell out. I stuffed them back into the outer pocket of the bag, and pulled out some coins. "Andi, keep this for me till I come back. It's stuffed so full of crap I need to re-arrange it or something." I handed it to her and went to the vending machine. When I put the coins into the machine and pulled the appropriate knob, nothing happened. I pulled it again. "Come on. Give me the feed." I slapped the machine.

Andi looked over at me. "What's wrong?" she called.

"I don't know. It just won't work."

She came to the machine and pulled her dark hair back as she peered into the opening. "It might be jammed or something."

"I guess I can try again. Give me some change out of my purse."

Andi's mouth rounded in an "O." "Oops. I left it over there." She put a hand to her mouth. "I'm sorry. I'm not used to--"

I shook my head. "Never mind. It's still there." I saw Drew squatted beside where it sat, holding his hand out to the goat. I went back to him. "Son, I don't know if we're--"

He grinned up at me. "Drew feed him."

I looked at the goat. Sure enough, he was chewing away.

"What did you feed him?"

He looked back to the goat. "Drew feed him," he repeated.

Andi appeared at my elbow. "What's up?"

I shrugged and picked up my purse. "I don't know. Drew says he fed the goat something." I dug through the junk in my purse. "Can we get change somewhere. I don't--" I stopped. "My money's gone. I had about eight dollars in here and it's gone." I set the purse on the ground and removed some of the larger items. "It was in here when I went to the machine the first time. I had a five, and I think about three ones."

"Drew feed." He pointed to the goat.

I stopped what I was doing and eyed the goat, then Drew. "Oh, no. You didn't feed that goat Mommy's money did you?"

"I feed," he said, and his black eyes crinkled at the edges.

"Julia! He used a pronoun we haven't taught him yet," Andi said. She scooped Drew up and danced around in the muck. "Far out, Munchkin. I feed, I feed!"

Startled by the noise, the goat took off. "Come back here, you," I said. "Andi, that goat's got my money. I know he does."

She set Drew down. "I'll get him."

She took off after the errant goat, dark hair flying. She almost caught him at the first turn, but lost her footing and had to grab the wooden fence to stop her fall.

Several people in the petting zoo stopped what they were doing to watch Andi chase the goat. Drew clapped his hands and jumped up and down. "Andi doing?" he asked.

Howard stood near John and Marie, and watched open mouthed as Andi streaked by. "You doing your dissertation on the cud-chewing mammal's response to stress, or what?" He laughed at his own joke, and a chunky woman with three kids in tow gave him a "Gee-I-hope-it's-not-catching" look as she edged away from him.

Howard grinned at her. "Ph.d humor," he said.

Andi ran by, close on the tail of the goat. "Help me," she panted.

The next time she came around, I stepped out in front of the goat in an attempt to head him off. The terrified animal ran across my feet and nearly knocked me over.

At that instant, Andi took a flying leap at the goat as it ran into the open stable-like building.

Drew and I walked toward the stable, followed by most of the people in the petting zoo.

Andi stood, breathless, her dark hair in disarray, with a firm grip on the goat.

"I've got him, but I don't know where your money is. I guess he really did eat it."

"Ate it?" Beside me, John and Marie giggled.

"A goat ate Mommy's money, a goat ate Mommy's money," John chanted.

I looked at the goat again. Now it was chewing on something. I tried to pry its mouth open. "Come on, open up," I said. "Open!" My loud voice must have frightened the poor animal, because he opened its mouth. Out fell one of the most disgusting messes I had ever seen. "What is that?" I asked.

Andi peered at it. "It looks like a hairball."

Marie pointed. "Look, Mom, it's got money in it."

"It's a cud," announced Howard.

"A what?"

"A cud. You know, like cows. They eat something, swallow it, then bring it back up and chew on it."

"Ew, yuck, vomit," Marie said, her nose wrinkled.

"That's disgusting," Andi said.

Howard shrugged. "Don't tell me, tell the goat."

I looked at the mess lying on the ground. I could see bits and pieces of green in it. "The damned thing ate my money," I said. By now a group of people had gathered.

A man in a shirt with Los Angeles City Zoo over one pocket pushed his way through the crowd. He looked at the goat, who by now rolled its eyes and uttered pitiful sounds.

"What's the problem?" he asked.

"That goat ate my money."

He looked at me. "He what?"

"Ate her money," Andi said. She pointed to the ground. "There it is."

The attendant removed a soiled handkerchief and wiped his glistening forehead. "Now I've heard it all," he muttered. He replaced the handkerchief. "I don't think we've ever had this happen before, but I'm sure we can take care of it." He went to a small building just outside the fence of the petting zoo and returned with a plastic bag. He picked up the goat's cud and put it in the bag. He held it out to me. "Take this to the accounting office. It's in that gray building over there." He motioned with his head.

I took the bag with my finger tips and held it away from me. "I don't guess they'd just take my word for it?"

The attendant shook his head. "Believe me, Lady. For this, they ain't gonna take nobody's word." He wiped his head again. "As a matter of fact, I better call 'em and tell 'em what happened myself."

I sighed. "All right." I looked at Andi, Laurie and Howard. "Do you guys want to stay here?"

Howard shook his head. "No way. You're going to need witnesses." He grinned.

"Ew, Mom," Marie said. "Are you really going to carry goat vomit around? That's gross."

"Eight bucks is eight bucks," I said.

We all trooped over to the indicated building, and found the accounting office. A receptionist greeted us with a cautious smile. "May I help you?"

I held up the bag. "A goat ate my money," I said.

"So I hear." She stood and walked around her desk. "Come back here. You need to talk to Brian."

We went through a door marked "Accounting." A man with glasses stood behind a desk as we entered.

"Brian, this is the woman Hector called about."

"Right." He looked at me. "So we have a criminal in the petting zoo, huh?"

I held out the bag. "Seems that way."

He took the bag and laid it on his desk, then went to a cabinet in the corner and brought back a roll of paper towels. He layered several on the desk, then dumped the mess in the plastic bag on them.

"I can't believe it," I said. "Are you actually going to pick out all the pieces of the money?"

His forehead wrinkled. "Well, sure. How else will I know how much to give you?"

"I can tell you now it was eight dollars."

He looked at me as he would an idiot child.

"Oh, all right," I said. "Go ahead."

While we waited, he began to pick out pieces of bills from the cud.

"Do we got to stay in here all day?" John asked. "I don't want to. I want to see the monkeys and the hoppa--hoppa--" He stopped and looked at Marie.

"Hoppa-pootamus," she said.

"Not either. Mom, she said--"

Andi broke into the conversation. "Julia, do you want us to go on to see the monkeys, and you can come over when you're finished?"

"I guess," I said. I was dying for a cigarette, and wished I could leave, too.

About ten minutes after they left, the bookkeeper looked up with a grin. "All done," he said.

I counted the bills. A five and two ones. "That's only seven dollars," I said. "I had eight."

He indicated the pieced-together bills. "I don't know what to tell you. I can only give you what I can see." He laughed, and made a snorting sound through his nose. "Maybe he kept the change."

"Yeah. Right," I said. "Just give me the seven dollars."

I stuck the five and two ones he gave me in my purse and turned to leave. Behind me, I heard the bookkeeper chuckle.

"Maybe he kept the change," he said in a low voice, and laughed again. As I neared the door, he called to me.

"Ma'am?"

I turned. "Yes?"

"I guess he really got your goat, huh?" His own joke tickled him so much that he collapsed in his chair, emitting snorts of laughter through his nose.

. . .

"I am told your trip to the zoo was a great success," Dr. Lovaas said the following Monday.

"Yes, it really was." I lit a cigarette. "I realized later that night that it was the first time since Drew began to walk that I've actually been able to take him anywhere without being afraid he would get lost or something." I looked to where Andi and Howard sat with Drew, drilling him on pronouns.

Dr. Lovaas smiled at me and inclined his head sideways. "The difference in him is remarkable, is it not?"

"Like night and day," I said, and felt myself begin to choke up as I considered how close my child had come to living a life of institutional routine.

"He becomes more like a normal child with every passing day, does he not?"

I nodded. "He really does."

Dr. Lovaas clasped my hand in both of his. "I am glad to hear you say so. It is time for him to begin preschool, and I do not want you to worry about him."

I bit my lip. "But--"

Dr. Lovaas stood. "No. No buts. You say yourself he is better and better. We must not let fear come between Drew and the next logical step in his recovery."

I sat silent as Dr. Lovaas walked away. He's probably right, I thought, but cold fingers of fear gripped my heart. Though Drew had made tremendous strides in the previous months, I couldn't shake the feeling that pushing our luck could be dangerous to him. What if the "next logical step" turned out to be one step too far?

Chapter 15

EXCERPT FROM PARENT THERAPY LOG

April 24, 1975

Drew started preschool today. When I handed him his lunch box at the school and told him it was time to go, he seemed to know. He took his teacher's hand and went in. I'm afraid--for both of us--but I'm also beginning to get excited about it now.

April 25, 1975

When Andi and Howard came out for the session yesterday after preschool, we couldn't wake Drew up. Today, he was very cranky, saying "No" to everything. I hope this isn't a bad sign.

"Okay, Big Guy," Dr. Helmann said. He lifted Drew from the examining table and stood him on his feet. He pulled a balloon from his pocket and handed it to Drew. "Here you are, my friend."

Drew took the balloon and ran to the door. He turned and looked at me. "Going?"

I looked at Dr. Helmann. "We need just a few more minutes," he said. He pulled a stool up to the built-in desk on one side of the examining room. "We need to complete this form for the preschool." He pulled a pen from his pocket. "Let me see. Drew's three, right? What's his date of birth?"

"January 5, 1972." Drew came to my side and tried to pull me by the arm toward the door. "In a minute, Son," I said.

Dr. Helmann ran me through a series of the usual background questions and finished by asking, "When did he begin to talk?"

"In March."

He lifted his shaggy white head to look at me. "March when? What year?"

"1975," I said.

The doctor laid his pen down. "What do you mean, March of 1975? That was last month. He was better than three years old."

"I know how old he was. That's what I've tried to tell you for the past two years. Drew is autistic, and until he started therapy, he spoke exactly five words." I had trouble reigning in my anger at Dr. Helmann. I didn't just want to say, "I told you so." I wanted him to know the pain he had caused me and my family by refusing to listen to me.

Now, he began to quiz me, in earnest this time, on various aspects of Drew's development. With each answer, his eyes widened a little more. Finally, he ran out of questions. He looked at Drew, who now swung on the door knob, his feet held off the ground and the deflated balloon clenched in his teeth.

Dr. Helmann moved his gaze from Drew to me. "It may be that I owe you an apology, Julia. Perhaps I was a little quick to attribute your fears to you being a nervous mother."

Since Drew entered therapy, I often had thoughts of how it would feel when the medical establishment finally recognized its mistake. "I told you so" had rang in my head then, but now I was surprised to feel only a small ray of smugness penetrate the well of gratitude within me. No matter what had or had not happened, I was thankful that Drew had received treatment, and that the treatment worked.

Dr. Helmann watched Drew perform an intricate series of steps while hanging on to the doorknob and humming to himself. Finally, he handed me the form. "He's all set, Julia. Whatever you're doing with him, keep at it."

. . .

I pulled up to the converted two story house that was home to Four Square Gospel Preschool. Andi waved to me from the front door and bounced down the steps toward us. "Hey, Munchkin," she said, and scooped Drew up. "Are you ready for this?" She planted a large, noisy kiss on Drew's forehead and stood him on his feet.

He lifted his lunch box toward her. "See?"

"Brought your lunch, huh? Good for you. This is going to be great." She pulled her dark hair behind one shoulder and looked at me. "Still nervous?"

"A little," I said.

Andi gave me a quick squeeze. "He'll do fine. Trust me."

"I still don't see why I can't stay with him." The fact that Dr. Lovaas and Andi refused to let me accompany Drew to preschool was rapidly becoming a sore point.

"Because mothers don't go to preschool with their children," Andi replied in a firm tone.

I lit a cigarette with shaking hands. "Neither do therapists."

Andi looked at me with undisguised amusement. "You just can't stand not to be in there with him, can you?"

"You're always saying I'm to get involved. Pitch right in, you say. ALL your best mothers do, you say. Well, what am I? A mother right? So why can't I--"

"Oh, now. You stop that. You're just nervous about him being away from you. That's normal, but you've got to mellow out, Julia." She shook her head, as if she had expected more of me. "This is a very important part of his therapy, and it just happens to be a part you can't be personally--"

Just then, the door opened and a red-haired woman in her mid-thirties peeked out, then came onto the stoop. "Hi, there. You must be Drew."

Drew looked at me, then Andi, and finally back to the woman. He held up his lunch box. "See?" he said in a small voice.

The woman held her hand out. "Would you like to come in? We're going to paint in a little while. Do you like to paint?"

Drew looked back at me. As much as I wanted to pitch a fit and insist I be allowed to accompany him, I didn't. I smiled at him and nodded. "It's okay. Go on," I said, and my voice shook.

He stared at me for a long moment, as if to store my image in a file in the back of his mind. Finally, he turned, took the woman's hand, and went into the building. I let out a pent-up breath.

"See?" Andi said. "He's going to do great. I promise. And I'll be right here with him."

I nodded, but my chest felt as if a lead weight were on it. "Yes. I'm sure he'll be fine." I wasn't sure though. What might be ordinary separation anxiety in another child could very easily throw Drew back behind his wall of silence.

At home, I paced and smoked and waited for time to pick up Drew. For the first time since his birth, I was completely alone, free to do whatever I wanted for the next four hours. I took a book out to the patio and tried to sit still.

"Caring For The Autistic Child" was a study in despair. It described four autistic children of varying ages, all of whom fell far behind Drew developmentally. Child A, it said, was seven years old and was not yet toilet trained, could not dress himself, and communicated with no one. I strained to concentrate, but finally threw down the book in frustration.

I went back into the house and paced aimlessly through it, leaving cigarette smoke, ashes and an aura of fear in my wake. What if Drew perceived my leaving him at preschool as abandonment? Couldn't he return to his former non- communicative state? "He needs me with him," I whispered to the empty house.

When I arrived back at Foursquare to retrieve Drew at 2:30, he clutched his lunch box and sat on the front stoop with Andi, who waved as I pulled up in the circular drive.

I scrutinized Drew's face, which seemed a little drawn and weary. Before I was fully out of the car, I began to quiz Andi. "How did he do? Did he play with the others? Did he cry for me?"

Andi stood and shook her head. "He did pretty well for his first time. He painted, and played alongside the other kids, but not really with them. He is interested in all the action songs they did--he imitated most of the actions." She smiled down at him. "He got a little whiney, but that's normal. He sure wasn't the only one."

I wiggled my fingers at Drew. "Come on, Son."

He stood, but didn't take my hand. Instead, he wandered out onto the grass and walked aimlessly for a few moments, then headed toward the fenced-in play area.

"No, Drew. Come on," I called. "We don't have time to play now." He ignored me and broke into a trot. At the swing set, he dropped his lunch box and threw himself belly down across a swing.

Andi laughed. "I guess he doesn't want to leave."

"Guess not," I said, and felt a little peevish. I thought he'd miss me more than that. "Come on, Drew," I shouted, and walked toward the play yard. He turned from the swing set to look at me, then ran to the jungle gym.

"Drew! Stop!" I commanded. To my intense relief, he did. I approached him and took his hand. As we passed his lunch box, I picked it up and tried to hand it to him, but he refused it. I looked at Andi. "He's acting like he did when he first started treatment. I thought starting preschool was supposed to be progress."

Andi walked toward me. "Come on. He obeyed you, didn't he? Any kid who is left for the first time in a strange place is going to react some way. It's natural." She stopped in front of me and put her hand on my shoulder. "Don't worry so much."

I was embarrassed at the tears I felt burn my eyes. "I can't help it," I choked out.

She hugged me, then held me at arm's length. "I know it's hard. Just have faith, okay?"

I wiped my eyes with the back of my hand. "I'll try." I sniffed back tears. "I guess you and Howard will be at the house later?"

She nodded. "We'll be there. 'Bye, Munchkin." She ruffled Drew's blond curls.

His brows drew together and he stared at the sidewalk in front of him.

Despite my promise to Andi, Drew's behavior scared me. As I hustled him to the car, I felt panic threaten to overwhelm me. "Don't do this, don't do this," I chanted under my breath. It was so like the "other" Drew, the one who was like the children in "Caring For The Autistic Child." So what if he obeyed me? He could still be regressing.

On the way home, I squeezed back tears as Drew rocked beside me in his car seat. By the time we made it to the house, he was asleep, his curly blond head at an uncomfortable angle. I gathered him up and carried him into the house. He didn't stir, even when I dropped my keys on the sidewalk and bent awkwardly to retrieve them.

Andi and Howard arrived a short time later. "Where's my little Munchkin?" Andi asked. She dropped her fringed leather bag onto the coffee table.

"Asleep. He nodded off before we even got home." I went down the hallway to the boys' room. Drew lay curled into a ball in the middle of his bed. I sat down beside him and smoothed his hair back from his forehead. "Come on, little boy. Time to wake up."

He didn't stir. I shook him. "Come on, Drew. Andi and Howard are here." When he still didn't move I shook him again. "Come on, now. You have to wake up." This time, he open his eyes and looked at me, then squeezed them shut again.

I sighed. "Okay. Have it your way." I picked him up, but he stiffened and I lost my hold. He fell back onto the bed. "All right, now, cut it out." I got a better hold on him this time, and managed to carry his stiff body into the living room. I stood him on his feet, and he crumpled to the floor in a heap.

"Well, what's this all about, Big Guy?" Howard asked. He squatted beside Drew and began to tickle him.

Drew slapped at him and buried his face in the carpet. "No," he said.

I shook my head. "He's been like this ever since I picked him up." One part of my mind looked to Andi for reassurance, but another part looked for a confirmation of my fears that Drew had slipped backward into autism.

Andi knelt beside Drew and sat him up. "He's just a little stressed. It's not serious." She sat him up. "All right, Munchkin, we're going to work whether you're ready or not."

Despite her words, we accomplished little. Drew refused to cooperate, and reprimands slid off him like rain drops off a waxed car. Nothing we did or said made the slightest change in his behavior.

"I think that's enough torture for one day," Andi said from her seat on the floor near Drew. She fell onto her back with arms spread.

"You think we pushed him too hard?" I asked. "I mean, if even you think of it as torture for him--"

Andi made a face at me. "Who's talking about him? I meant me. I'm exhausted." She sat up and nodded toward Drew, who sat with a scowl on his face. "He's doing just what he wants to do. We're the ones wearing ourselves out."

I looked at Drew. He face seemed pinched and somehow unhealthy looking, and at that moment, I wished more than ever that I had not allowed him out of my sight.

That night as I lay awake beside a sleeping Gene, unanswered questions circled in my mind like vultures over carrion. I couldn't stand the thought that I might wake up some morning to find Drew holding a deck of cards in his hand, running his thumb over their edges and reciting numbers, but neither could I find within me the faith that he would one day live a completely normal life.

I looked over at Gene. He lay on his back with his mouth slightly open. I wanted so much to wake him up and ask him to hold me, to tell me that Drew would be fine, our marriage would survive, and mostly, that I was not alone with my fears. Even as these thoughts ran through my head, I knew that the support I needed would not come from Gene. It had to come from within me.

When I finally drifted off, my sleep was punctuated by dreams of a helpless Drew, alone and anchorless in a black sea beneath a sky the color of hopelessness.

Chapter 16

Despite my apprehension, Drew adjusted well to preschool. I watched him day by day in a constant flux between amazement at his progress and fear of his regression. I couldn't seem to find a comfortable middle ground. All the hope and faith I had held for his complete recovery had deserted me at the first major turn--his entry into preschool.

About three weeks after he began preschool, I heard the sounds of a heated argument coming from the boys' room.

"It's my turn to go to school," I heard John shout.

"No! Not neither. My turn. I going to school today," Drew returned.

The sweet sound of my sons squabbling as brothers do was like an aria performed by angels. It served to liberate me from the prison of foreboding I had built for myself. As I lay listening, a smile began to tug at my mouth and exultation suddenly blossomed inside me. Drew would make it. Dr. Lovaas and Andi, Howard, and the other therapists had given me the tools to work with, and as long as there was breath in my body, I would use them.

With those tools, I would make certain that my son overcame every hurdle as he came to it, and nothing would stop him. In that instant, standing in the hallway listening to the sounds of sibling rivalry, I knew as surely as I had ever known anything that Drew would have the life every child deserved.

Chapter 17

The next year passed in much the same way as the first six months of therapy had. As a family, we were busy with school, church and other activities. John and Drew were both well settled in their respective regimens, and Marie seemed to have become a professional Girl Scout.

As the summer of 1976 drew near, I sensed closure in two important areas. Drew's therapy was nearly complete, and the end of my marriage was imminent.

Never one to give up without some semblance of a fight, I sought counseling for our marital problems. I asked Gene to attend the sessions also, and he refused. I felt very angry at not only his refusal, but also his lack of support during Drew's therapy. I knew that in order to overcome the anger, I would have to put some distance between Gene and me.

We came to a mutual decision to divorce, but agreed to keep the household intact until Drew was released from therapy.

Ivar and the therapy team gradually decreased the time Drew spent in therapy. That time now became filled with preschool and other activities. Drew acted more and more like any other four-and-a-half-year-old.

When I announced to Ivar and the team that I would be returning to my hometown in July, it seemed to come as a shock. They were certain by now that I was equipped to handle any problem that might surface in relation to Drew's treatment, but what had begun as a working relationship had become a close friendship. I knew Ivar, Andi, Howard and the others would miss us, as we would them, but I felt that returning to Oklahoma was best for the children as well as me.

For my last activity as co-leader of Marie's Girl Scout troop, I agreed to chaperon forty Girl Scouts on a tour of the Queen Mary. The huge ship was docked in Long Beach, and our trip promised to entail a full day.

Drew and John accompanied us, and both were enthralled with the sights they saw on board. Drew in particular found fascinating some sort of large gun. It had a seat on it, and he insisted upon being placed there for a few minutes. When we continued with the tour, he could not stop talking about the big gun. Though I felt his progress in therapy to be phenomenal, he still sometimes exhibited the single-minded, narrowed focus of the autistic child when something special caught his attention.

"Go big gun, 'kay, Mommy?" he implored.

"Not now. If we have time later we will, but there is a lot more to see," I said. I nearly had to drag him along with us for the next hour. Every new sight was punctuated by a plea to return to the big gun.

At noon, we left the ship to eat our sack lunches. As we began to eat, I noticed that John was without the light summer jacket he had left the house with.

"What did you do with your jacket?" I asked.

John's eyes widened as he looked around him. "I don't know. I think I left it on the boat." He started to rise. "I better go find it."

I put a restraining hand on him. "No, you can't do that. You'll be as lost as your jacket." I stood and lit a cigarette. "I'll go report it to the security office. Come on, Drew."

As we started for the security building, one of the mothers stopped me. "Julia, you can leave Drew here. That's kind of a long walk for his short little legs."

I looked down at him. "Well, I don't know. You have to watch him really close. He tends to slip away when you least expect it."

She laughed. "Don't be such a worry wart. I've got kids, too. I can handle it."

"Okay. I guess it will be all right." I looked at Drew. "You stay here and eat your lunch, and do what Myra says, okay?"

He bobbed his blond head. "Okay, Mommy," he said, and bit into his peanut butter and jelly sandwich.

I found the security building, and reported the missing jacket. When I returned to our group 15 minutes later, Myra ran to meet me.

"Oh, Julia, Drew's gone."

My heart sank to my toes. "How long has he been gone?"

Myra twisted her hands. "I don't know. Not very long. I'm so sorry, Julia. It's like, he was here, then he was gone. Just like that."

"I know," I said. "It's not your fault." I sighed and tapped a cigarette on my thumbnail as I scanned the grounds. I spied a red shirt in the distance and cupped my hands around my mouth. "Drew!" I shouted, and ran toward him. When I got closer, I could see that the child in the red shirt was not Drew. With the other mothers' help, Myra and I searched the grounds. Finally, I gave up. "He must have gone back to the ship. I'm going to go to the security office again."

I trotted back to the building that housed the security office. As I entered, an officer seated at a desk held up John's jacket. "Somebody turned it in right after you left."

"Thanks," I said, and took the jacket from him. "Now I've got a bigger problem." I explained Drew's disappearance and described him. "I'm sure he's gone back to that big gun. That's all he's talked about all morning."

"You're probably right," the security officer said. He picked up a two-way radio and spoke into it, then looked at me as he replaced it on his desk. "Someone's checking that area now."

"Thanks," I said. I started for the door.

"Ma'am? You need to stay here in case we find him."

I turned to face him. "But he's probably at that gun. I can find that."

He shook his head. "No, ma'am. What usually happens is we find the child and lose the mother. If you'll just have a seat, I'm sure they'll have your boy here in no time."

I reluctantly sat down and watched the minutes tick by on the big wall clock. Before long, John entered the room, followed by Myra. A pack of little girls and mothers peeked around her into the security office.

"Any luck?" she asked.

I shook my head. "Not yet."

She hesitated. "Well, the thing is, it's getting kind of late, and we do want to finish the tour --" She broke off and gave me an apologetic look.

I felt like an abandoned child, but I nodded. "Fine. I'm sure he'll turn up shortly, and we'll find you."

She left, and John climbed up on my lap. "Myra said Drew is a slippery little booger."

"He is that," I said. Another ten minutes passed, and every nerve in my body seemed exposed.

Finally, the phone rang. I listened to the one-sided conversation, and my fear increased. The officer cradled the phone and shook his head.

"I'm sorry," he said. "They still can't find him."

I felt perilously close to tears and perched on the edge of my chair, John still on my lap. Another fifteen minutes passed, and the phone rang again.

This time, the officer smiled when he hung up. "Bingo!" he said.

"Oh, thank God," I said. "Where was he?"

The man blushed. "The last place we looked."

"The big gun."

He nodded. "The big gun. Not only that, but it wasn't our staff who found him." His face, neck and ears became even more red. "His sister and some other Girl Scouts found him."

I laughed aloud, then hastened to apologize. "I'm really sorry. I just can't help it. If you only knew --"

Drew's bubbling voice interrupted me. He ran into the room, followed by a gaggle of girls. "We found him by that gun thing," one of them said.

I stood John on his feet and approached Drew. "Why did you take off? We were so worried. Didn't I say-- "

"Big gun, Mommy. I find it myself." He beamed at me, thrilled with his accomplishment.

My heart wasn't in the scolding I gave him, but it was as integral a part of the treatment as praise and reward were. Still, the delight on Drew's face was precious to me, and even while I scolded him, I savored his joy as a thirsty man does water.

. . .

The move back to Oklahoma was as uneventful as I could have hoped for, considering the circumstances. I found Drew a good preschool and a baby sitter for John and Marie. It seemed that all Drew's problems were behind us. I still had to work with him, but not as intensively as in the past.

I stood at the kitchen sink washing dishes one day shortly before Drew was to begin kindergarten. I watched him absent-mindedly for a few minutes as he sat in the back yard. He had crossed his legs Indian style and was rocking vigorously back and forth. Suddenly, I snapped to attention. He was self-stimming! He hadn't done that in months. With a scream, I dropped the plate I was washing and bolted out the back door.

Chapter 18

Stop!" I shouted.

Drew stopped instantly, a frightened look on his face. I knew I had scared him, but he had scared me more. Marie tore around the side of the house.

"Mom! What's wrong?" She looked from me to Drew and back again. "What is it?"

"Play a game with Drew, Honey. Any game. I've got to call Andi."

"Is he okay? Is something wrong?" Her small face looked pinched and worried.

"I'll explain later, Marie. Just keep him occupied." I ran back into the house and dialed the clinic at UCLA. When Andi came on the line I was nearly hysterical.

"I just caught Drew self-stimming, Andi. What are we going to do?"

"Calm down, Julia. What was he doing?"

"Rocking. Oh, God, I knew I shouldn't have brought him back here. What was I thinking?"

"Now hold it. It's all right. What did you do when you found him?"

Her measured words seemed to calm me a little, and I took a deep breath. "I ran out and yelled 'Stop!' Then I had Marie play a game with him."

"Okay. That was exactly the right response. Can you see him now?" she asked.

I pulled the phone as far into the kitchen as it would go. "Yes."

"All right. What is he doing?"

My breathing seemed to return to normal. "He's playing with Marie."

"No rocking?"

"Not now."

I heard Andi release a breath. "Great. You see? You handled it exactly as it should have been handled. Everything's cool now." She paused a moment as if thinking, then resumed. "I'll talk to Ivar, and one of us will get back to you tomorrow. Are you going to be okay?"

I stared out the window at Drew and Marie. "Yes. I think so."

"All right. We'll get back to you. Try not to worry."

I tried to heed her advice, but remained on edge until Ivar's phone call the next day.

"And how is Drew now?" he asked. His calm, accented voice transmitted confidence to me long distance.

"He seems fine. I'm just afraid for him. He hasn't self-stimmed in so long." I lit a cigarette and inhaled deeply. "I'm afraid," I repeated.

"Of course you are," he soothed. "It is quite natural after all you have been through. But you cannot help Drew by worrying."

"I know."

"You handled the situation precisely right. You can be proud of that. Now, you must simply wait and watch. If the behavior occurs again, we will fly out and see to him."

By the time we hung up, I felt more confident of my abilities. Still, I watched Drew carefully and instructed the employees at his pre-school facility to be watchful also.

. . .

By the time Drew began school, I was also attending. At 37, I decided to seek a degree in learning disabilities. Once more, the children and I moved, this time across the state.

I don't know whose success in school I worried more about -- mine or Drew's. I began my third semester at the same time Drew entered kindergarten. Because of his participation in the Young Autism program, certain criteria had to be met, one of which was that he had to get through first grade without anyone realizing that he had developmental problems of any sort.

During that year, Drew slipped away from his teacher three times. Each time, I found him on the door step of our apartment, a short distance from school. And each time, I prayed for him to develop the fear of being lost that other children had. That prayer was answered in the summer of 1978.

We went with a group of other parents and children to Six Flags over Texas. While there, I left Drew with the others while I went to buy refreshments. When I returned, the others were looking for him. The child seemed to have radar that detected the exact moment that someone's attention wandered from him, and he always took advantage of it.

We set out to find him, and I was both aggravated and worried. I felt there was no need to check with the station near the front gate where lost children were brought. Drew had no fear of being separated from me, so he never appeared to be lost, and chances that he would be at the gate were quite slim as far as I was concerned.

Finally, we had exhausted every other possibility. "We may as well at least check by the gate," I told the others, and we all trooped back through the huge park. As we approached the station, I heard a child's sobs above the other noise and I knew at once they were Drew's. As I ran toward the station, I saw him. He stood with a Six Flags employee, who was trying in vain to quiet him.

I claimed him and picked him up. "I was lost, Mommy. I couldn't find you," he sobbed.

Even as I comforted him I grinned. I knew that would be the last time he disappeared.

Once we returned home, I began preparing Drew for first grade. It would be the most important year of his life so far.

Chapter 19

My nervousness about Drew's real "criteria year" seemed to rub off on all of us as the school year started in 1978. We all seemed to be on edge as the fall semester began, but we quickly settled into a routine.

The first nine weeks went well for Drew. During the tenth, I receive a note from his teacher that she would like to have a conference with me. Filled with dread, I called and made an appointment with her.

That evening, I watched Drew where he and John sat in the middle of the living room floor building a structure with Lincoln Logs.

"Drew?"

He looked up. "Huh?"

"Do you know why Mrs. Rogers wants me to come and talk to her?"

He shrugged and snapped another log in place. "Maybe she just likes you."

"Somehow I doubt that," I said.

"Maybe Drew is going to get in trouble," John suggested.

"No, I'm not." Drew scowled at his brother. "I do good at school."

"Of course you do. John's just teasing you," I said.

I tossed and turned through the night and was up before the alarm went off. I fed and dressed the kids, and we all went to school.

My appointment was for 3:30, and it seemed to take forever to get there. I arrived fifteen minutes early, and stood outside the school building smoking. Finally, I took one last puff and put my cigarette out.

Mrs. Rogers was a pleasant young woman who seemed to truly enjoy her work. We took seats in chairs far too small for us, and I couldn't wait for her to begin. "What is it? Is Drew having some kind of problem?"

She smiled and patted my shoulder as if I were one of her charges. "Not at all," she said with a laugh. "I just have a couple of questions for you." She looked down at the file on her lap then back to me. "As you probably know, Drew is quite a talker."

I nodded. "He can be."

"Well, some children are more talkative that others, and sometimes those children can be a little disruptive. I've had to speak to Drew several times about talking to the other children when they should all be working. Do you know what he said to me the last time?"

"I can't imagine," I said, insides churning.

"He told that I ought to be glad he was talking at all, and that it took a lot of people to teach him to talk." She tilted her head to one side and waited for my reply.

"Why, that little smart aleck," I said weakly. "I'm still not certain why you had me come in."

"I just thought there might be something you needed to tell me about Drew. I need to know if something is wrong," she said.

"Well, I--that is, uh," I began. "Do you think there's something wrong?"

"No, not particularly. It's just that Drew said it took a lot of people to teach him to talk, and I just thought any speech therapy should go in his school records. Other than that, he seems like a normal little boy who likes to visit with his classmates a little too often."

I tried to keep a straight face, but was only partially successful. "Yes, you're right. He's a perfectly normal little boy," I said.

When I left Mrs. Rogers' first-grade classroom that day, I felt as if I were walking on air. It seemed funny to me the power that words held over us. Three years previously, my son had been barely able to communicate. He could not use words to tell us how he felt, or where he hurt. To explain his condition, we were introduced to the word "autism." With it came fear and uncertainty.

The therapeutic process had been grueling, and I had learned to use the words "behavior modification," prompt," and "modeling" in the context of therapy. Words such as "regression" and "self-stimulation" brought with them dread and apprehension. On this day, another word, "normal," was spoken. With it came joy and hope, and the certain knowledge that what had begun in tragedy had ended in triumph.

Chapter 20

Today, Drew is twenty-one years old, and a student at a state university. His life is very much like that of any other young man of his age. He spends his time studying or socializing, and finds particular pleasure in attending country music concerts. He's always the one in his crowd to spend the night on line at the ticket office to make sure of getting the best seats.

Drew doesn't remember much of his time in therapy, and seems to take his normality for granted. I don't. Even today, many years after his autistic behavior was extinguished, I find myself watching Drew, seeking opportunities to further his socialization.

There are an estimated 350,000 autistic individuals in the United States today. Not every one of them will be as fortunate as Drew was in finding help. Not every single child in the Young Autism Project had the success that Drew did. However, a great many of the participants in the program have been very successful, and are today leading full and healthy lives because of Dr. Ivar Lovaas and those who have and do work with him in this area.

The most important thing a parent can do for his or her autistic child is to persist. Make your complaint heard, regardless of how many professionals you must call on.

When you do find help, realize that how far your child progresses is going to depend largely on you, the parent. Public institutions cannot be counted on to provide everything your child needs to go forward. It is imperative that the parent support the chosen program by providing additional training at home and by eliciting cooperation from friends and family members so that they may become teachers, too.

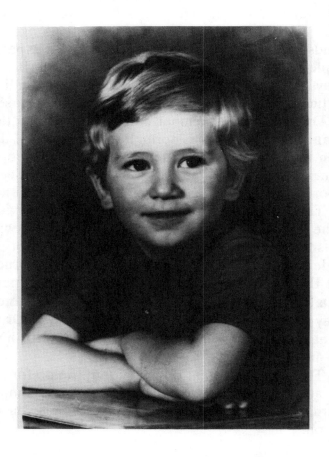

Afterword

The following is an essay written by Drew for a psychology class during his second year of college.

Me

Every person has a story, and this is mine. The three main subjects I will touch on are who I am, where I am going, and how I will get there.

I am sort of a quiet person who can get a little loud when I get in certain moods such as anger. Also, I have a tendency to be absent-minded and careless. After my sixteen-year-old cousin was killed in a junior rodeo, I have been a little more quiet and conservative, and it also made me realize that at any time, anyone can pass on.

My family and friends basically have the same values. We all believe in our country, stand by our opinions and beliefs, believe in being friendly to everyone we meet, and we believe in God. Our religion is the root for our opinions and ideas and even though we differ on some issues we basically agree on just about everything. We are a close knit family and even though we are spread from Idaho to Florida . . . it doesn't mean a thing.

Among the things I like to do are bowl, play pool and play baseball. If I could have one day to do anything I wanted, I would sail the Pacific on a giant yacht, lay out in the sun and party all night. However, I might fly to Monte Carlo and gamble and blow a bundle of money and have nothing to show for it except a good time.

Right now, I have no idea where I am going in life. I do have plans, like my plans for this week are to get all my homework done and to, hopefully, find a part-time job so I can earn some extra spending money. I also want to get on a solid sleeping schedule and fix the transmission leak in my car and fix the timing belt on my mom's car. It is easy for me to plan a week or two in advance even though I really don't do it that often.

My plans for the trimester are to have a 'B' average and to show up regularly for class. My main problem in high school was attendance. My grades would have been a lot better if I had just shown up for class. It took me forever to figure out that attendance is one of the keys to success in school. My other problem in high school was lack of studying. During my senior year I was either at school, working, or sleeping.

I do hope to get married someday and to have a nice home out in the country and to have children. Right now, however, that seems way off in the future. The main things in my personal life right now are friends, family, and having a good time while I'm still young. I would like to better myself through my friends, school and hard work. Additionally, the most important thing to me in the future is to have a normal, happy, and enriching life.

I love biology. Who knows, I may even go pre-med. For the moment my goals are to get my basics out of the way with a good grade point average and see where I am at that time. I really don't care where I work as long as it pays good and it is something I enjoy doing. If a person doesn't like their job they don't do that job as well as they could.

The way that I would get there is with hard work, perseverance, and dedication. If you want to achieve certain goals in life there are no short-cuts.

My physical attributes include: reflexes and patience. Overall, however, I am not a good athlete even though I played high school baseball for two years. I don't believe that athletics is important to succeed in my field, biology. A person does need some muscle coordination since it is used in almost every job. When I was seven years old, I broke my wrist in two places, which in turn destroyed a bunch of my fine motor control. This is the reason I never became a very good athlete.

As for my mind, I am good at math, science, and history because my memorization skills are good. On the other hand, I am not very good at artistic or creative things like painting or poetry. I know my intellectual limitations and have set my goals to fit into those limitations. My feeling is, if you are not very good at something how can you enjoy doing it?

I have a solid education. Once I reached high school, I started to explore the full range of subjects. My freshman year was basic high school courses, but when I became a sophomore, I started taking higher level classes, My junior year I took chemistry and Spanish and I found out what I was good at when I made an 'A' in chemistry and nearly flunked Spanish. When I was a senior, I took advanced biology, math and journalism and my grades in these courses proved once again what my strong and weak points are in school. In college I intend to improve on my artistic skill while maintaining an interest in biology.

I do have trouble expressing my feelings to others. The main reason I believe is that I have a linear thought process. I don't know why I think like this because my mom, brother, and sister are very emotional. I do express my emotions in extreme cases. For example, when a family member dies or when one of my friends gets screwed. There is a good side, however. The fact that I am not very emotional helps me in every decision I have to make. In some situations it hurts but overall it helps.

I do like to meet new people but I'm usually too shy to start a conversation. I do feel fairly comfortable around other people. I've been to so many parties that it doesn't really bother me any more to be among the crowd. When I finally start a conservation with another person I do enjoy it. The fact that I am shy doesn't mean I hate talking to other people.

I hope this paper helps you to understand who I am, where I am going and how I am getting there. My feelings and ideas my change in the future, but doesn't everyone change over the years?

. . .

Therapy such as that Drew received while involved in the Young Autism Project is just the beginning of recovery. The most important instruction one can impart to the parent of an autistic child is "Never give up." If you don't find an answer for your child the first place you look, proceed to the next, and the next and the next, until everything that can be done has been done. Above all, know that there is hope. There is hope for your child because of the children who have gone before him or her. There is hope for your child because of the parents who have gone before you. There is hope for your child because of Dr. Ivar Lovaas and others like him who saw that within the autistic child, there may be another child who can be coaxed out by persistence and, ultimately, the right treatment program. When it seems that there is nothing to hold on to in your search for your child's wholeness, hold on to this: There is hope.

Glossary

Autism -- An illness distinguished by inability to respond to others but being excessively involved with things. Symptoms can include extreme food fads, repetitive behavior, apathy, fear of change, and often a total inability to use language to communicate. These behaviors become apparent within the first three years of life.

Behavior modification -- Changing behavior through a step by step system of reinforcing desired behaviors and eliminating undesired behaviors. The system is based on the methods and findings of behavioral science.

Childhood schizophrenia -- An illness similar to Autism but beginning after the age of three and involving a loss of development rather than a failure to develop.

Discrete trial -- Command or request which has a clear beginning and a clear ending and is made of a person undergoing therapy.

Auditory discrimination -- The ability to differentiate sounds or words.

Empirical data -- Facts and figures which are based upon experimentation.

Modeling -- Teaching new behaviors by means of imitation.

Peabody Picture Vocabulary Test -- A receptive language test that shows several pictures. The tester says a word and the person being tested should point to the proper picture.

Prompt -- Physically assisting someone to complete a requested act.

Refrigerator mother -- Term coined by early researchers to describe the typical mother of an autistic child. Some believed that autism was the fault of the mother, an idea that has been discarded.

Regression -- A loss of acquired skills.

Retarded -- Failure to develop mental capacity for education and socialization that is expected of the general population.

Self-stimulating behavior -- Any of a variety of repetitious behaviors performed by an autistic person.

Tantrum -- A fit of temper.

Verbal cue -- A word or phrase that serves as a signal for a specific response.

Vineland -- A test to determine the developmental level of a person by interviewing the person's caretaker(s).

Bibliography

Lovaas, Ivar O., *Teaching Developmentally Disabled Children--The Me Book*

Lovaas, Ivar O., and Leaf, R.B., *Learning* Videotapes

Index

Ackerman, Andrea 4, 55-61, 73, 74, 76, 79-82, 86
Bowling For Dollars 88, 89
California 12, 24, 51, 54, 119
Cantara Street School 130
Cheerios 14
Children's Hospital 114, 118, 119, 122
Cream of Wheat 14-16, 18
Doug 42, 73-77, 81, 82
Formica 14
Franz Hall 54, 61
Girl Scouts 165, 168
Green Eggs and Ham 39
Howard 4, 55, 104, 115, 116, 133, 134, 137, 142-144, 148-150, 152, 153, 158-160, 162, 165
Jack-In-The-Box 43, 45, 59, 60, 74-78
Jello 42
Kanner 7, 69, 94, 95
Ked 15
Kirk 41
Laurie 4, 30, 55, 60, 86, 88, 89, 91, 92, 94-96, 98, 123, 124, 126, 133, 134, 143, 150
Lincoln Logs 87, 174
Lindley Street 26, 28
Lovaas 3-5, 11, 12, 33, 36, 42-45, 48, 50-56, 59-61, 65, 66, 69, 70, 72-83, 86,

88, 90, 94-96, 133, 152, 155, 162, 177, 183
Lucky Charms 101
Medix 18, 21, 25, 29, 30, 34, 44
My Favorite Martian 87
Norway 60
Oklahoma 119, 165, 169
Paula 42, 43
Peabody Picture Vocabulary Test 184
Pop Goes the Weasel 74, 77
Queen Mary 165
Reseda 72, 99, 104, 116, 117
Rolling Stones 99
San Diego 11, 64, 93, 122
Scandinavian 54
Schreibman 18, 22, 29, 30, 32, 34, 36, 38, 44
Sears 132
Sesame Street 25
Seuss 39
Simmons 46-53, 55, 69
Spock 24, 41, 92
Star Trek 92
Tonka 106
TV Guide 20, 58, 135, 137
University of California 12
Vineland 56, 185
Young Autism Project 11, 12, 33, 45, 47, 70, 80, 177, 182

BOOKS ON HEALTH-RELATED ISSUES

AIDS READER--Documentary History of a Modern Epidemic by Loren Clark and Malcolm Potts is an anthology on the history and impact of AIDS by some of the world's great experts. Paper, ISBN 0-8283-1918-9, $17.95.

ALZHEIMER'S--A Handbook for the Caretaker by Eileen Driscoll, a nurse with several decades f experience, gives hope to those having to cope with alzheimer patients. Paper, ISBN 0-8283-1962-6, $12.95.

AUTISM--From Tragedy to Triumph by Carol Johnson and Julia Crowder--the mother--tells the story of a young man, from birth to college matriculation. Paper, ill., ISBN 0-8283-1965-0, $12.95.

HINDU PSYCHOLOGY--Meaning for the West by Akhilananda explores, in clear style, the impact of Hinduism on the West. Paper, ISBN 0-8283-1353-9, $14.95.

MAKING WISE CHOICES--A Guide for Women by Charlotte Thompson, M.D. contains a series of essays on crucial issues confronting women--married or single, especially those who may have to make it alone. Paper, ISBN 0-8283-1972-3, $12.95.

MARIJUANA--Up-Date by Dr. Richard Robbins presents extensive research done by civilian and military personnel on the use and abuse of this drug. Paper, ISBN 0-8283-1856-5, $11.95.

MENTAL HEALTH AND HINDU PSYCHOLOGY by Akhilananda has become a classic in this field. Paper, ISBN 0-8283-1354-7, $14.95.

PARKINSON'S--A Personal Story of Acceptance by Sandi Gordon is the autobiography of Sandi as a woman, a mother and patient suffering from this dreadful and common disease. Illustrated. 1949-9 $12.95 p.

PUMPKIN--A Young Woman's Struggle with Lupus by Patricia Fagan--the mother and professional nurse--tells the story of 'Pumpkin', and her relationship with relatives and friends. Paper, ISBN 0-8283-1961-8, $12.95.

SINGLE SOLUTIONS--Essential Guide for the Single Career Woman. Charlotte E. Thompson, M.D. It gives information especially aimed at the single professional woman. This 1933-2 $11.95 p.

YOUR BABY'S SECRET WORLD--Four Phases for Effective Parenting by Larry Cheldelin, M.D. presents mothers with information gathered through many years of medical experience and research. Paper, ill., ISBN 0-8283-1850-6, $9.95.

At your local stores, or,
directly from the publisher:
Visa-Master Card orders only: **1-800-359-7031**
(Postage and Handling: $3 first book, $1 each additional book).